When Good
Isn't Good Enough

Also by Ron Willingham

*Integrity Selling: How to Succeed in Selling
in the Competitive Years Ahead*

RON WILLINGHAM

When Good
Isn't Good Enough

Doubleday

NEW YORK   LONDON   TORONTO   SYDNEY   AUCKLAND

Published by Doubleday, a division of Bantam Doubleday Dell Publishing
Group, Inc., 666 Fifth Avenue, New York, New York 10103

Doubleday and the portrayal of an anchor with a dolphin are trademarks of
Doubleday, a division of Bantam Doubleday Dell Publishing Group, Inc.

Library of Congress Cataloging-in-Publication Data

Willingham, Ron, 1932–
When good isn't good enough
Ron Willingham. —1st ed.
    p. cm.
  1. Success. 2. Goal (Psychology) I. Title.
BF637.S8W5224   1989
158'.1—dc19   88-18739

FF

To my wife, Beverly

Wisdom is meaningless until your own experience has given it meaning.

—Bergen Evans

✱ See pg. 112 - Health Habit 1 Shaklee!

Knowledge w.o. experience is not wisdom!

Self-image = mental opion of self.

Get fired-up!

Not just read + know BUT practice + discover!
Success comes as we prepare to achieve it!
Practicing gets you experiencing + growing!
What 2 people will I talk to today?
What will I practice dynamically w. them?

Contents

Paradigm =
Parameters -

PART II

PART III

Preface

In 1974, during one of my hundred or so visits with Dr. Maxwell Maltz, plastic surgeon and author of the best-seller *Psycho-Cybernetics*, he told me this story while having lunch at the St. Moritz Hotel in New York City.

It began one afternoon when a widow from the Midwest, who'd read his book, called him with an unusual request. She explained that her husband had built a very successful grain business and had died prematurely, leaving her to run it.

She went on to tell the doctor that her husband's death had left her with a young son at home, as well as the responsibility of running their business. She had been strongly motivated, she said, because she dreamed of her son growing up and assuming the management of the business, thus keeping it in the family.

Then, she explained, her son had grown up, left home to go live in New York City, leaving her with shattered dreams. All of the pressure she exerted to get her son to move back to the Midwest and take over the business had no effect on him. He wanted no part of it.

The doctor interrupted her and said, "I don't understand . . . why are you calling me?"

"Because I want you to convince my son to move back here with me!"

"But, madam, that's your affair . . . not mine!"

She persisted and finally twisted Dr. Maltz's arm so that he promised he'd at least visit with her son.

In a few days the son showed up at the doctor's office in the eighteenth-floor penthouse at 57 West Fifty-seventh Street. He was noticeably embarrassed that his mother had set up the meeting.

The doctor, quick to get down to business, asked the young man, "Why did your mother want you to see me?"

Slowly the man began his answer.

"My father was a very strong man. Even stronger than my mother . . . and you know how strong she can be. Since the time I was very young, he tried to teach me to be strong and tough."

"What do you mean?" the doctor asked.

Taking a deep breath, the man replied, "Well, let me tell you this story. . . .

"When I was just a kid, my father played a game with me. We'd go out into the yard and he'd throw a baseball for me to catch. The deal was that if I could catch ten balls in a row I'd win the game."

The young man went on. "My father would always throw nine balls where I could catch them. . . ."

Then, pausing for a moment, he continued, "But he'd never let me catch the tenth ball! He'd throw it over my head, into the ground, or other places where I couldn't catch it. But . . . he'd never let me catch the tenth one!

"He thought he was teaching me to be tough and self-reliant . . . I suppose. . . .

"Doctor, I hated that awful game! And I hated him for doing that to me!"

The young man paused, gazed into space, and was silent a moment. Then he looked at the doctor and said, "That's why I won't go back and run a business that he built. Even though I love my mother, I won't go back. I can't live in his shadow. I've got to find a life of my own."

The doctor nodded his understanding to the young man.

Then the man summed up his whole story by saying, "You see, doctor, I've got to prove to myself and to the world that I can . . . that I can catch the tenth ball!"

Dr. Maltz wasn't his usual busy self that day. He ordered coffee after lunch and relaxed while we drank it. As he peered out the restaurant window at the people coming and going, he was silent for a few moments. Then he brought his mind back to the present and said, "You know . . . many people go through life never . . . never catching the tenth ball."

"Nor even *expecting* to catch it," I added.

He nodded, "That's right. Most people allow themselves

to be beaten down and stuck in an environment that they accept. They never even think of moving outside it."

I'll never forget the impact that experience had on me.

Many people *do* go through life never catching the tenth ball! Never really discovering the incredibly powerful, creative people they are.

That's what this book is about—about discovering your incredibly powerful, creative self . . . about catching the tenth ball!

It's for people who want to be high achievers . . . who want to be better, to accomplish more, and to enjoy greater levels of living . . . who are willing to take possession of their lives and explode through previous boundaries.

It's for you . . . when good isn't good enough!

Introduction

An infant reaches out for a colorful rattle, picks it up, and shakes it.

The evening before a big game, a professional baseball player, currently batting .400, mentally sees his bat connecting with every ball that will be pitched to him tomorrow.

A youngster gets on a bicycle that was a Christmas present, wobbles for a few feet, falls, gets up and tries again; and a while later he is able to ride the bicycle for a whole half block.

A man destined to be the world's best-known hotel owner carefully places a picture of the Waldorf Astoria under the glass on his desktop, and stares at it daily—fantasizing about actualizing this dream.

A housewife mixes flour with several other ingredients, kneads the dough, carefully places it in a pan, and visualizes how much the family will enjoy hot rolls for dinner tonight.

A person dashes into a department store for a quick purchase, immediately whiffs the inviting aroma of popcorn, visualizes how great it would taste, and, without thinking, buys a bag to munch on.

All of these people did the same thing.

"What?" you might ask. They set and achieved a goal!

Knowingly or unknowingly, they all used their inner Goal-Seeking Mechanisms to help them make things happen.

But the problem is that most people don't even know they have an inner Goal-Seeking Mechanism. No one's ever told them. And they sure didn't learn it in school.

So how can we use something we don't even know we have? You'll be excited to know that this book will answer that question. You'll learn about this incredibly powerful inner dimension you have. You'll also learn about the awesome power that awaits your discovery and use of it. But, more importantly, you'll learn how to harness this creative power to reach goals that are important to you.

Yes, I know that other books have been written about this subject. But you'll find this one is different.

For starters, I'll present these concepts in such a way that you'll understand them and find them fascinating. Next, I'll take you by your hand and walk you step-by-step through a simple process—simple but incredibly powerful. As a result, you'll reach some exciting new goals and enjoy new levels of self-fulfillment.

Why am I so certain this will happen?

I'm certain because I've presented my copyrighted Goal Achievement System to tens of thousands of people—through seminars, courses, books and articles for more than twenty years now. More than a half million people have gone through my courses. Thousands of other people have read my books and articles.

All this experience has convinced me that most people live well under their potential. I've also learned that all people, when they learn *how,* can enjoy goals that they never dreamed possible.

Now I realize that you probably don't *emotionally* believe what I've just said. But you *will* when you take action and follow the steps I'll give you in this book. Follow my instructions exactly and you'll discover for yourself that what I've just said is true.

I'm going to teach you how to make things happen! Of course, they will happen only if you have a high desire to learn and are willing to actually perform the steps I'll ask you to take.

Please challenge me and make me prove what I've just promised. Keep reading.

WHAT YOU'LL LEARN IN THIS BOOK

Here are four major benefits you'll enjoy when you *assimilate* and apply the information in this book.

1. You'll learn that you have a well-defined belief system that totally controls *all* your actions, feelings, behavior, and abilities.

2. You'll also learn that you have a built-in Goal-Seeking Mechanism. It's been given to you by your Creator to help you reach goals that are important to you.

3. You'll learn how to *program* your built-in Goal-Seeking Mechanism—how to use it to reach important goals.

4. You'll learn the following Goal Achievement System, which you can use for the rest of your life to reach any kind of goal you'll ever want to reach.

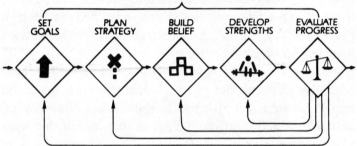

GOAL ACHIEVEMENT SYSTEM

SET GOALS — PLAN STRATEGY — BUILD BELIEF — DEVELOP STRENGTHS — EVALUATE PROGRESS

Pretty strong promises, aren't they?

I realize they are. I also appreciate your skepticism. My promises by themselves won't cause you to emotionally believe me, and you shouldn't. You should accept these ideas only after testing them to see if they'll work for you.

Now I need to be honest with you and tell you that merely *reading* this book won't give you these benefits. I don't want to mislead you. Simply reading this book won't help you. In fact, it may even frustrate you—if all you do is *read.*

But it can—if you carefully follow the directions I'll give you—be the beginning of increased success for you. When you take *action,* when you *recognize* success principles, *relate* them to your life, then *assimilate* and *apply* them.

At the end of each chapter, I'll give you some action guides to practice. When you apply them, you'll go from *knowing* to *doing.* You'll see results. Something will happen.

You'll discover that you suddenly begin to enjoy goals that have previously seemed beyond you. As you work through the action guides, you'll catch yourself unconsciously accepting new possibilities and expecting higher levels of achievement.

Yes, whether your goals are to be selected for your school play, pass a physics exam, discover an ability, earn more money, get a better home, have more confidence, or build a high-rise office building—you'll find this book helpful.

And here's another tip. Don't just read this book through and put it on a shelf. Read it like this:

1. Scan the whole book first to get an idea of its content.
2. Come back and spend one week reading and rereading Chapter 1. Read it, chew on thoughts, digest them. Underline ideas and write notes on the pages. Practice the action guides.
3. Then spend one week using the same procedure on each chapter.

At the end of twelve weeks, you'll have *experienced* this book and gotten several exciting benefits from it. You'll have developed some know-how and levels of awareness that will pay off in a big way for you in the future.

You'll look back and see that you've grown and expanded your own personal belief system. You'll enjoy the thrill of reaching goals that were previously unattainable. You'll see yourself, your possibilities, and your future with new expectations and vitality. Your actual achievements will expand to fit your new beliefs.

With this book as a guide, you no longer need to settle for less than high achievement!

Man is what he believes.

—ANTON CHEKHOV

What you think, you [LOOK / DO / A·R·E]

Part I

Everything has been thought of before, but the problem is to think of it again.

—JOHANN WOLFGANG VON GOETHE

1

Understanding Your Powerful Belief System

It was the summer of 1944. I was going to be in the seventh grade come September. My family lived in a small town in Texas. An event happened that had a lasting impact upon me.

But, first, let me back up and start from the beginning.

The biggest deal in the lives of the kids in my neighborhood was airplanes. We were all going to be pilots when we grew up. We could look at silhouettes of airplanes and tell you whether they were American, Japanese, German, or British. We could tell you how fast each flew, how many people they carried, what kind of machine guns they had, what size bombs they dropped—we could tell you *everything* about airplanes.

Our favorite hobby was to build model airplanes. There were two kinds of model airplanes—solid models and ones made out of balsa wood and tissue paper. The solid models came in a box, with parts, preshaped, where all you had to do was sand the pieces down, glue them together, and paint them. After doing this you'd have a finished, well-proportioned airplane.

The only problem was that it took almost no creativity to make them—as well as little time.

I remember saving my money and making a couple of these models. Then I got bored with the lack of challenge and decided to make the other kind. The other kind of model came in a much bigger box. Inside the box was a large pattern printed on a folded sheet of paper. There were balsa-wood strips that you cut out and glued on the pattern —making a fuselage, wings, tail, and rudders.

Then after the superstructure was made with balsa-wood strips, tissue paper was glued over it and painted. The objective was to have something that looked like an airplane.

Well, I'll never forget the *first* one I ever made. And . . . what turned out to be the *last* one, too!

I remember that it seemed to take forever to build the model. It may have been only three or four weeks—you know how time goes by so slowly when you're a kid.

Well, I finally finished it. And it was the most incredibly beautiful piece of work that I'd ever seen. Surely no one had ever built one that looked this good.

I can still remember just standing back and admiring it—having difficulty believing that I had actually done it.

I remember planning the unveiling ceremony—when I'd show it to my family. I carefully planned just the right moment—for maximum impact. As I planned the unveiling, I could even hear the applause I'd get—the raves. I even visualized all my friends and neighbors swarming in to gasp at the masterpiece I'd created.

So, one evening when my whole family was in the living room listening to our old Zenith console radio, I made my entrance. Inside me cymbals were clanging, trumpets blaring, and kettledrums banging!

I still remember how carefully I carried the plane so that I wouldn't damage it or drop it. I entered the room, beaming with pride, displaying the incredible creation that I'd done. And . . . if I live to be a hundred and one years old, I'll never forget the response I got.

Holding the airplane out and waiting for the accolades of the whole world to descend upon me—the response I got wasn't exactly the one I'd planned.

My father looked at the airplane, scrunched up his face, got this real pained look, looked at my mother and said, "Do you reckon he'll ever learn to make one *right?*"

I was devastated. Stunned. Speechless.

Immediately a big knot welled up in my throat, and I reacted the way I'd been conditioned to react in my family environment—I just stood there speechless, showing no emotion whatever.

And in the next few seconds I internalized that whole massive shock. It was as if someone had crammed a hand grenade down my throat, left it lodged somewhere between my throat and my stomach, and then walked away . . . then, in a few seconds, it had exploded.

I remember standing there, my emotional equilibrium destroyed, and then, without saying a word, walking out of the room. I walked outside, through the backyard to the alley, where we had large trash barrels. I remember standing beside one of them and pulling the lid off. I don't remember how much time went by.

After a while I ripped one side of the wing off . . . then the other. Then, piece by piece, I crumbled up the airplane and threw it into the barrel. After doing this, I eased the lid back on the barrel and walked away—as defeated as anyone could ever be defeated.

And here's the point of the story. Until this very day, over forty years later, I've never again attempted to make a model airplane. I never even considered it! It wasn't because I didn't *want* to make one. As I mentioned, airplanes were our greatest interest, and I desperately wanted one.

My point is that this experience *convinced* me that I *couldn't* do it. And it was as if I had no hands, no mind, no coordination, no desire—no nothing—I was just as bound! It had nothing to do with my actual abilities. It was all due to my negative beliefs. It was all in my own head. I even remember, a couple of years later, saving some money and paying a friend to make a model airplane for me. Not once did I consider making one myself.

Do you relate to this story? Most of the people I've told it to do.

WE ALL HAVE A VERY STRONG AND POWERFUL BELIEF SYSTEM

You see, the truth is that we all have a very strong and powerful belief system that has been formed by our responses to all our life experiences. This belief system is what we believe to be true about ourselves—what we believe to be true about our abilities and possibilities and about our world.

We all unconsciously examine our successes and failures, our good times and bad times, our joys and sorrows. As we mentally deal with these experiences, we make assumptions about ourselves. We unconsciously say, "Here's the kind of person I am. Here's what others think of me. Here's what I'm capable of doing. Here's how much I should earn. Here's the kind of people I relate best to. Here's the kind of neighborhood I should live in."

We make thousands of other assumptions about ourselves —mostly unconscious, mostly based on what we *perceive* as truth.

It's important to emphasize that this belief system has been formed by our *interpretation* of our past experiences. Truth or reality have little influence upon our belief systems. It's our *perception* of reality that molds them.

The power of our belief system was best summed up by Dr. Maxwell Maltz, author of the best-seller *Psycho-Cybernetics.* He wrote, "All our actions, feelings, behavior and abilities are consistent with our self-image. Our self-image is our mental opinion of ourselves."

The purpose of this chapter is to help you understand the power of your belief system. To look within yourself and discover how your actions, feelings, behavior, and abilities are (all) influenced by it. The purpose of this whole book is to help you use this knowledge in a creative way to reach new goals that are important to you.

THE POWER OF YOUR BELIEF SYSTEM IS ENORMOUS

The power of your belief system is enormous. It influences your choices, your decisions, your life direction. It influences the size and quality of goals you set. It influences the people with whom you associate. It influences the money you make and the neighborhood you live in.

It's interesting to think about how even subtle suggestions from others often cause massive impacts upon our lives by causing us to form certain beliefs about ourselves.

A physician stood up in one of my courses one evening and told this story. He said, "I'm a doctor today because of an accident I experienced when I was a child!"

He went on, "When I was a child I grew up on a farm. My whole family had always been farmers and had done hard, physical work. I was riding a tractor one day when I was nine years old. The tractor hit a bump and the jolt knocked me off; several bones were broken. They took a long time to heal.

"From then on I was spared from doing hard physical labor. I remember my mother saying many times while I was growing up that I would have to get an education and do something that didn't require hard physical work . . . like being a doctor. From then on I never doubted that I'd go to college and become a doctor."

Interesting example of the power of repeated suggestions

in influencing a person's belief system, isn't it? I'm fascinated by the almost insignificant events that impact people's belief systems and then guide them to major life experiences.

As I was writing this, I received a note in the mail from a young man about to enter medical school. He told me about going to school and ended his note by writing, "Just think, it all started at your seminar."

My mind went back about five years ago when I was conducting a two-evening goal-setting seminar. I met a man who introduced me to his son. The man's name was Norman Pahmeier and his son's name was Gene. Gene was about eighteen or nineteen years old, blond, very clean-cut, and good-looking.

I could sense some friction between the two. I later found out that Gene's father had dragged him to the seminar against his wishes. His father told me that Gene was listlessly laying around the house—not knowing what he was going to do.

After the seminar was over, I spent some time with him that first evening. I told him what a sharp young man he was and that he could really go places. He asked if he could come early the next evening and talk to me. "Sure," I replied.

I talked to him the second evening. I gave him a cassette album on goal setting to listen to. He sat in the front row and carefully wrote down some goals.

His father called me a few days later and said, "Boy, you really got Gene fired up! He's set a goal to go to college and become a physical therapist." Norman also told me that Gene had flunked out of school before I met him.

At this point he entered a university and went through

physical therapy school with honors—having about a 3.5 grade-point average. Now he's going to medical school.

Well, as I said, I'm fascinated by the almost insignificant events that impact people's belief systems and then guide them to major life experiences.

This was the case with me. For more than twenty years I've been involved in writing books, designing training programs, and conducting seminars. As I mentioned earlier, I've written more than twenty-five programs that well over a half million people have gone through. We've trained over sixteen thousand instructors to conduct these programs.

I've written self-concept programs for public and private school curricula, programs for banks, unemployed people, college students, church leaders, and many sales groups. I've designed courses to help people lose weight. I've written programs to help people sell cars and trucks with more integrity.

All this started from a single, almost insignificant experience. But one, I might add, that had a powerful influence on my own belief system.

It was in 1964 and I'd owned a small retail furniture store for about five years. I had supposed that I'd stay in that business for the rest of my life. We'd just built a new store building and I had a pretty heavy commitment. Then an event happened that doomed my business overnight!

About half our sales were to officers at a nearby air force base. We had a Strategic Air Command unit there. They made good incomes and moved around a lot . . . so they went through furniture pretty fast.

One morning our local newspaper headlines blared in bold print: MCNAMARA ORDERS BASES CLOSED.

It then went on to say that ours was one of the bases

targeted to close. I knew this was bad news, but I didn't know how quickly the bad news would influence us. From that day on, we never sold a dime's worth of anything to air force people. Nothing! Our business stopped literally overnight!

As the next few months went by, hundreds of homes were dumped on the market. Most of the home builders either moved out or went broke. Vacancies appeared everywhere. Our business was going right down the tubes, and I didn't know what to do.

In desperation, I did something I'd never done before. I bought a self-help book. It was entitled *Success Through a Positive Mental Attitude* by Napoleon Hill and W. Clement Stone. I read it several times trying to really understand its message. I enrolled in some courses the National Retail Furniture Association offered. I took other personal-development courses—searching for something.

Then one day a family moved to town. The man was to be the new minister at the church where we went. His name was Joe Barnett, and I was awed by him immediately. He was a bright, classy guy who had high goals and a great way of building people. They bought some furniture from me, and we became good friends.

One day we were visiting and talking about self-help books and personal growth, and he said, "You know, one of the greatest needs we have in the church is better leadership."

He thought for a moment and then made a simple statement that was to totally to change my life.

He said, "As interested as you are in personal development, I'll bet you could design a leadership training program and conduct it at the church!"

It was an incredible moment. I'll never forget it. Bells chimed. Whistles blew. Fireworks went off.

For some unknown, totally illogical reason, I thought, "Hey, if he thinks I can do that, he must see something in me that I don't see in me."

So based purely upon his expressed belief, I spent about six months putting a leadership course together—all because I thought *he* thought I could do it. The materials were very homemade and amateurish and my facilitation was pretty rough, but it worked. We saw people's lives change. Marriages improved, some people got job promotions, some increased their incomes, others gained the confidence to speak in public.

I'll never forget conducting the first session. I fumbled and was terrified. My knees shook. My stomach churned. I couldn't even remember the name of the course when it came time to begin the first session. But the class members gave me a lot of support and encouragement, and I felt like I'd just conquered the world.

I had stumbled through it. And . . . what an experience.

The next morning after hardly sleeping at all, I woke up feeling like I'd never felt before. I felt different—exhilarated, excited, awed at what had happened the night before. I went to the store before the other employees arrived and just sat there thinking—reflecting on the evening before.

I can't describe the feeling. It was as if my whole future were displayed before me, as if God were saying, "Look quickly, because I'm going to give you a glimpse of things to come!"

What a strange feeling. I suddenly knew exactly what I

wanted to do with my life. I knew that I'd be very good at it. I knew that lots of people's lives would be influenced.

But what I didn't hear God say under his breath was, "But it ain't gonna be easy!" After experiencing some of the difficult times that followed, I'm sure He must have added this little addendum.

Within the hour I decided to liquidate the store, lease out the building, and begin conducting leadership courses full-time. I called my friend, Joe Barnett, to lay this exciting news on him.

I didn't know it then because he didn't have the heart to be honest with me, but he was terrified. *What have I done to mess up this person's life?* he thought to himself, caught in the trap.

Luckily for me I couldn't see the risks and problems ahead. I was so excited that I thought things would simply turn out wonderful. It never dawned on me that I was risking my whole future. I had no idea of the struggles I'd have or . . . the thrills!

Then one day several months later, I was visiting with my friend again. He said, "You're going to need to become a good writer. Why don't you take a correspondence course called the Famous Writers Course?"

"Me," I thought, "a writer?" It didn't make sense. I couldn't write. I had done so poorly in English in high school that I had to take English five days a week my freshman year in college. I never could understand the difference between a gerund and a gerbil. I still don't know exactly where to put commas.

But, hey, if he thought I could become a writer . . . man, that was OK with me! "Where do I sign up for this Famous Writers Course?" was my next question.

So I enrolled in the course. It was a correspondence course, and I had to send in writing assignments. I was so motivated to learn that I devoured the whole course. It got me into writing and analyzing books and articles that were well written. I was excited and fascinated with the possibilities of becoming a writer.

To look back at the beginning of this massive change in my life just blows me away every time I think about it. The impact of Joe Barnett's encouragement on my own belief system changed the direction of my whole life. This caused me to really begin understanding the power of my beliefs.

"WHATEVER THE MIND OF MAN CAN CONCEIVE AND BELIEVE, IT CAN ACHIEVE!"

In that first self-help book I bought and read, authors Napoleon Hill and W. Clement Stone kept repeating the suggestion, "Whatever the mind of man can conceive and believe, it can achieve!"

I must admit I had to read that over many times before its full impact began to seep into my understanding. Then I learned that there's a big difference in intellectually accepting a cliché and emotionally internalizing it. And quite frankly, I'm still learning new levels of meaning of that statement.

It fascinates me to think about the Mystery of Mental Chemistry, which can cause one person to be a superachiever and another, with apparently similar skills and abilities, to fail miserably.

I've written a training program for Chevrolet called *Chevrolet's Integrity Selling*. One of the reasons they had me design the program was the high turnover of salespeople in their dealers' organizations. Some dealers experience over 100 percent salesperson turnover a year, and many salespeople sell an average of only eight to ten units a month. But recently I visited with Larry Merritt in Atlanta, who sells fifty to sixty units each month.

Why does he sell five times the number of cars and trucks that most salespeople do? He isn't five times as intelligent, nor does he work five times as many hours. The reality is that he *believes* he *should* sell fifty to sixty units a month. He *expects* to perform on that level. He *thinks* in those terms. And since he believes, expects, and thinks he can . . . he does! He performs on that level.

Why can you look around and spot people you went to school with, who made higher grades than you, did better in athletics than you, had a lot more going for them than you did—yet their achievements have gone downhill since then and yours have gone uphill? Or vice-versa? Why?

Why is it that we can experience a dozen successes and one failure, and that one failure will have a negative impact on our achievement for years to come? And we apparently forget the dozen successes. Why?

"Whatever the mind of man can conceive and believe, it can achieve!"

HOW THIS BOOK WILL HELP YOU

This book will help you several ways. First, it will help you understand the power of your own belief system. Not intellectually . . . but emotionally! Not by *reading* words and then *knowing*. But by *practicing* ideas and then *discovering!*

You see . . . the secrets of high achievement are well

hidden from those who aren't seriously seeking them. High achievement comes to us indirectly. It doesn't come as we understand information. It comes as we *prepare* ourselves to *receive* it!

I'm not writing this book to give you information. You can read it from cover to cover and still receive no benefits from it. That's a fact! Or you can read it a chapter at a time and stop and *apply* the suggestions. You can take a few ideas and *practice* them. This subtle difference will spell the difference between gaining only a little or benefiting a lot.

In each chapter I'll present a basic concept. Then I'll give you some action guides to practice. Practicing these action guides will get you *experiencing* and *growing*. This isn't a passive learning process; it is an active, dynamic, success-promoting activity.

Follow my direction, and you'll achieve goals that are important to you but have heretofore been out of reach. You'll discover some strengths about yourself that have never surfaced before. You'll get new, larger glimpses of your possibilities. You'll begin to discover the *essence of* achievement—the most *essential element!*

ACTION GUIDES TO FOLLOW

Here are three simple steps that will prepare you to benefit most from this book. Take some time and perform these actions before going to the next chapter.

1. Write down three or four of your own life experiences that popped into your mind as you read this chapter.
2. Ask yourself, "What did these experiences cause me to *believe* about myself and my abilities?"

3. Then ask yourself, "Now that I can look back with a fresh perspective, were my beliefs based on truth or falsehood?"

What this reflection will reveal, if you're like most people, is that some of your self beliefs limited you. They frustrated you. They caused your confidence to erode. They did because they were based on falsehood not truth.

I want to look directly in your eyes and tell you that the truth about you is that you are creative and capable of high achievement. The potential is already within you—it's always been there—it was put there by your Creator. Think about this and it will cause you to examine your current beliefs and see if they're based on truth or falsehood, and then to begin to sort out the exciting truth about yourself.

This bit of introspection can be extremely creative—it can help you feel much better about yourself. It can help you discover the truth about yourself. It can help you see yourself in an entirely new way.

SUMMING UP

Each of us has a well-defined belief system, formed by our *perception* of our past life experiences. Your belief system controls all your actions, feelings, behavior, and abilities. These are the two main points I want to make in this chapter.

In the next chapter, you'll learn how to change your self beliefs. You'll also learn that when you change them, your actions, feelings, behavior, and abilities will change automatically.

And then in the other chapters you'll learn how to set success goals . . . and achieve them. You'll learn how to use your Creative Mechanism. You'll learn how to add meaning and purpose to your life—to go beyond goal achievement.

Be sure to come back and read this chapter as I've outlined. Underline points, make notes in the margins. Look for success principles. Then take action and *apply* the principles you discover.

I don't want you to just read this book—I want you to experience it!

2

Expanding Your
Mental Paradigm

For about ten years, as a hobby, I conducted training
courses for a college football team. The objective was to
help them have more confidence and increase their abilities.
As a result, we saw changes in some of the players that
bordered on the miraculous.

One of the skills I taught them was to mentally picture
what they wanted to physically perform. Along with relax-

ation techniques, I'd have them visualize themselves executing their moves and plays exactly as they'd like to do them physically.

One of the young men was also a high jumper in the spring. One day, as I was talking to him, he told me how frustrated he was with his jumping. His coach had told him that he should be jumping six inches higher than he was able to do. His jumping had leveled out, and he couldn't seem to raise the height, even though he very much wanted to.

He was a very serious young man and had a high ability to concentrate. In talking to him, I felt he was tensing up and trying too hard, and this frustrated his performance. I talked to him for a few minutes about programming his mind and then letting it take over and influence his physical skills.

I gave him these instructions. First, to go out to the jumping pit and place the bar at the exact height he'd *like* to be jumping now. Then to back off a few yards, sit down in the grass, and for several minutes just look at the bar.

After this he was to relax, breathe deeply, close his eyes, and visualize himself sailing over the bar. I asked him to be very specific and mentally notice every detail of his imaginary jump. To see himself run up, plant his foot, clear the bar with his body, and kick his trailing leg over it.

SPEND TWENTY MINUTES EACH DAY IN MENTAL PREPARATION

He committed himself to spending twenty minutes each day doing this mental preparation. Within three or four weeks he had increased his jump six inches and was reaching an exciting goal for himself.

It's interesting to note that his height, weight, muscle tissue, and physical condition hadn't changed at all. Then what released the ability to perform at a higher level?

The obvious answer is that his belief system was expanded, and his performance took a corresponding change. It was cause and effect! His belief, or mental picture, was the cause. His performance, or apparent skills, were the effects. Everything is cause and effect.

Understand this profound concept and you'll begin to understand how you change. How you can make more money, have a larger home, get a better job, have more friends, learn new skills—or reach any other goal that you set.

As you grapple with this concept and as you learn by experiencing the guides I'll give you in this book, you'll peel off layer after layer of self-inhibiting attitudes. You'll then see greater and greater possibilities for yourself.

But now, for a few minutes, let me elaborate on these concepts. Stay with me, slow down as you read the next four or five pages. Read carefully because I'm going to lead you through a discovery process that can immediately project you into new levels of achievement.

YOUR MENTAL PARADIGM

Let me introduce you to the word *paradigm*. You pronounce it "para-dime."

This interesting word, *paradigm,* has several different meanings—as many of our words do. Sometimes the word means a model, a form, a boundary, a border. I'll use it to mean a boundary or a border—a line that encompasses an area. So the term *mental paradigm* would simply refer to our mental boundaries or borders—the line that outlines our own belief systems.

We each have a mental boundary or border. This mental boundary, although unconscious, powerfully controls all our feelings, actions, behavior, and abilities. Everything we do, achieve, have, or accomplish is consistent with this inner belief system—this mental paradigm.

Now let me stop for a moment and say that if you understand what I've just written, you know something that most of the people who've ever lived didn't know. And even the greatest of our thinkers have never probed to the deepest levels of understanding it.

Let me present this concept graphically so you can understand it easier.

WE FORM OUR OWN BELIEFS ABOUT OURSELVES

First, let's begin with the truth that we each *unconsciously* evaluate all our life experiences—our successes, our failures, our moments of despair, our moments of ecstasy. Then based upon our own perceptions of the kind of people we are—be our perceptions true or false—we draw a circle that forms our own inner belief system.

Let's say that this X represents me in my world.

X

As I go on through life evaluating my experiences, I make all kinds of assumptions. Remember, these assumptions may be based on truth or falsehood. I unconsciously say to myself, "Here's the kind of person I am." Or "Here's how I perform." We then plot how good we *perceive* we are or how well we perform in our environment.

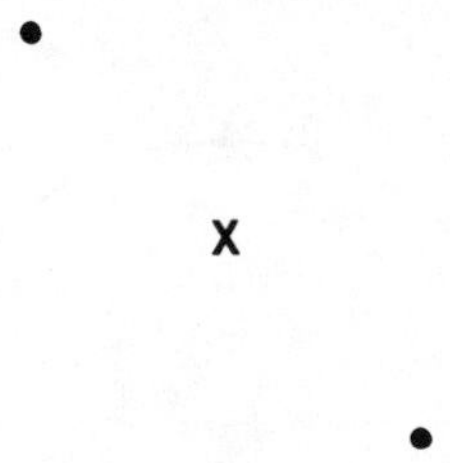

•

X

•

We unconsciously say, "Here's what certain people think of me." We make other assumptions. We say, "Here's the kind of job I can do." "Here's where I should live." "Here's the kind of home I should have." "Here's the value system I should have." "Here are the kind of people I best fit with."

We make thousands of these unconscious assumptions about ourselves, our world, our relationships with other people, our environment, our possibilities. And with each assumption, we unconsciously plot where we perceive ourselves to be.

Look at it like this.

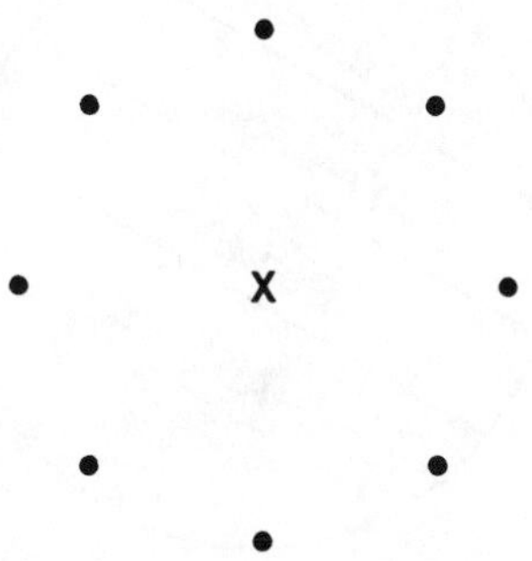

•

•   •

•   X   •

•   •

•

If we could plot these thousands of unconscious assumptions we make about ourselves and then connect them, we'd form our *mental paradigm*—our mental boundary, or border, like this.

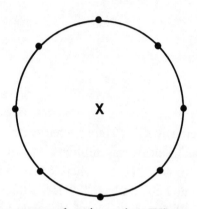

And here's my second major point. Whatever this mental paradigm, or belief system, is, it controls and regulates all our actions, feelings, behavior, and abilities. Our performance will not go beyond the limits we unconsciously place on ourselves.

Let's look at this drawing for an example.

Our inner belief system is so powerful and profound that
we literally can't act inconsistently within it. Attempts to do
so only bring failure and frustration. Not only that, but
pressure to go beyond our mental paradigms causes discomfort and disorientation. We stoutly resist any attempts to
make us act in a way that is inconsistent with this incredibly
strong inner belief system—this mental boundary.

Since this is true, it's helpful to know that all personal
growth begins by increasing our mental paradigm; and we
usually do that in small increments. As we expand our belief
system, our actions, feelings, behavior, and abilities *automatically* expand to fill it.

It's like this.

As we begin to understand all this, we may bump our
foreheads with the heel of our palms and exclaim, "My
goodness, this is why most so-called motivation fails! It fails
because it attempts to change people's actions and levels of
performance without first changing their belief systems—
their mental paradigms!"

STOP AND REFLECT A MOMENT!

Now stop for a moment and reflect on what I've written so far in this chapter. As you think about this powerful concept, some natural questions arise:

What have my experiences caused me to believe about myself?
How many of my beliefs are based on truth and how many on falsehoods?
In what ways have I underestimated myself?
Can I change my own mental paradigm?
If I want to do so, how can I change it?

Let's think of some answers to these questions. Let's think of some specific actions you can take to expand out your belief system—thus automatically causing your performance to change.

In order to introduce some action guides that you can practice, let me tell you a story I think you'll find interesting. It's not a normal story, and you may not even believe it. It is true, though, and it powerfully illustrates how well-established paradigms can be changed.

Marvin Daniel was principal of Alabama Christian High School in Montgomery, Alabama, and a certified instructor of one of my nine-week courses. He scheduled a course for high school sophomores once a week for two hours after school.

A couple of weeks before he was to begin the course a woman came and talked to Marvin about her fifteen-year-old son. She told him that her son's name was John, that he was severely retarded, and that he would eat and talk only around his immediate family. She explained that John had been to all kinds of child psychologists and the verdict was always the same—there was nothing that could be done for him because he was incapable of learning.

She asked Marvin if she could bring John and just have him sit in a class of young people his age one afternoon each week—just to be around them. She explained that she didn't expect him to learn anything, but she wanted him to have the social contact with the other kids.

Marvin gave her permission, with a couple of stipulations. One, that if John caused any disturbance, he'd have to be withdrawn. Two, that she'd allow him to test John. She happily agreed.

Then Marvin remembered the course he was about to begin, and he asked her if he could enroll John. He explained more about the nature of it, and again she agreed.

At the first session Marvin explained the course benefits and then had the kids come three at a time to the front of the room and tell their names and what they wanted to gain from the course. He told John that if he didn't want to say anything it would be okay. All the kids introduced themselves and were applauded. To Marvin's surprise, John wanted to talk after the other kids did. In a halting, difficult-to-understand way, John gave his name and said that he'd like to learn how to talk to other kids. Sensing that John was different, the other kids applauded him, and Marvin showered him with recognition and praise.

At the conclusion of the session the kids voted on the Desire Award—for two people who showed the most desire to gain from the course. John won one of the awards. Marvin said that when he presented the book award, John was emotionally touched. Apparently he had never experienced this kind of recognition and positive reinforcement,

After the session ended, Marvin took John out to his mother's car, wanting to explain what had happened and how John had won the award. His mother could hardly believe that he had actually spoken around the other kids. Then when she learned that he had also eaten a cookie and drunk a soft drink with the other kids during the break, she was almost speechless. That had never happened before.

The weeks rolled by. John was receiving tremendous amounts of praise and recognition in the course and outside. Marvin, especially aware of the situation, went out of his way to notice him and show his concern for him. The teachers did also. The other kids seemed to sense his needs and responded with lots of attention. They wrote him notes of encouragement during the week.

Slowly, John began to communicate. When he did, Marvin began testing him, and some strange findings began to emerge. First, he found out that John had an understanding of math. He could do some math problems, and understand certain mathematical concepts. Now, remember, he'd never been to school or communicated with a teacher. Marvin brought in a high school algebra teacher who sat down with John, and to their amazement he understood some of the concepts.

They were astounded! No, completely stumped, is more apt. There was absolutely no explanation for what was happening.

John progressed through the nine weeks of the course. His social skills gradually expanded. When he began communicating, the teachers learned more and more about him and were able to draw him out.

One of my staff people went to their Session Nine Awards Banquet at the Holiday Inn in downtown Montgomery. The twenty-five kids had brought their parents and had selected a spaghetti dinner.

Our staff person, Paul Tarence, a part-time speech teacher at Alabama Christian College, told me that what happened at the banquet was an experience he'd never forget.

After dinner each of the kids came to the front and took two to three minutes to tell what they had gained from the course and how it had helped them in their lives. John got up before some eighty people, and when he finished, Paul said, there wasn't a dry eye in the room—especially John's parents.

In a quiet, slow manner John told that he'd learned to talk to other kids, that he'd discovered some abilities he had, and had made some new friends. No one seems to remember what he said after that. They were all so overcome with the happy emotions that resulted from seeing this supposedly retarded young man pour out thoughts that had previously been blocked.

Marvin kept me informed about John for a year or so. He entered a special school that could better deal with his problems. He learned to drive and got a driver's license. He got a part-time job. They found out that he had some rather remarkable talents and abilities. He became more self-reliant and able to do things for himself.

It all seemed like a miracle. And in a sense, I suppose it was. But if it was, the miracle was in the releasing and not in the inner potential. The inner potential had been there all along. It was just waiting for the right stimulus, or catalyst, to bring it out.

This new environment—the love, support, and encouragement that John had received—was the dynamic that he needed to expand his paradigm and release the creativity that was inside him all along. Somehow, we suspected, both he and his parents had believed the evaluation of professionals early in his life that he was severely retarded. The fact that he had some problems wasn't to be denied, and he'll probably never be a totally normal person. But his whole life changed because of this paradigm shift he experienced.

Now, you might be thinking (even if you believe my story) that this is a rather extreme example and that you would have difficulty identifying with it. I realize you can't identify with it—at least literally. But figuratively we can all identify with it. We can because we all have allowed people, circumstances, past experiences, and our environment to convince us that we can perform only in a limited way. John suddenly came into contact with people and circumstances that helped him discover that he could perform in an expanded way.

MOST PEOPLE LIVE WELL BELOW THEIR POTENTIAL

The tragic truth is that most of us get locked into accepting a role in life that's far below our potential. We allow ourselves to believe falsehoods about ourselves. We let circumstances convince us that we're not adequate. Without protesting, we conform to the small paradigms that we unconsciously form. The sobering fact is that our paradigms are of our own making and can be changed. I am totally convinced of this possibility after working with thousands and thousands of people in training courses. We don't have to live limited lives.

As it's so powerfully put in the scriptures, our Creator did not give us a spirit of fear but of power and love and a sound mind. Any positive view of a Divine Creator suggests power and possibilities. Being created in the very image of God suggests a transfer of this power. To deny our own power is to deny this great gift from God. To acknowledge and use this gift is to glorify and prove our appreciation to Him.

To consider that God's very Spirit has been breathed into me as a Creative Force, along with the fact that I have a choice whether or not to use it, combined with my belief that the Spirit opens doors and gives me guidance—all these considerations present enough food for thought to keep me continually trying to understand all this. And . . . my understanding changes often, too!

We'll deal much more with this spiritual dimension in later chapters.

WE HAVE THE POWER TO CHANGE!

The case I want to build is simply this: We have the *power to change!* We have the *power to become.* I believe this power is given to us to help us expand our lives, as well as the lives of others. The question is, then, "How do I go about changing?"

ACTION GUIDES TO PRACTICE

There are other ways to change our inner belief systems, but let me give you three action guides to practice that will get you started. When you practice these, and mix in some time, your inner beliefs will begin to change.

1. Listen to people without bias. Search for truth without preplanned outcomes.
2. Each day examine all your strengths and weaknesses and be thankful for both, and ask for guidance for learning from both.
> 3. Choose a success environment—select people, places, and things that support the person you want to become.

Listen to People without Bias!

Listening to people without bias isn't easy, is it? And it isn't natural either. The reason is that we get locked into a womblike paradigm that's warm and comfortable and safe.

To hear anything that contradicts our assumptions is disturbing. When information or ideas are presented to us that are inconsistent with our way of thinking, we reject them. We may even attack them or try to discredit them. We do so because they disrupt our emotional and mental stability— our personal comfort level.

I must warn you . . . listening without bias can be very disruptive—both to you and to those who want to control you.

Examine Strengths and Weaknesses and Be Thankful for Both!

The second way to expand your own mental paradigm is to examine all your strengths and weaknesses each day and to be thankful for both, and to ask for guidance for learning from both.

Here's a quote I found over twenty years ago. When I found it, I had just gone through a deflating business reversal. I typed it on an index card and hung it above my credenza. It was written by William Law.

Here's what he wrote:

If anyone could tell you the shortest, surest way to all happiness and perfection, he must tell you to thank and praise God for everything that happens to you. For it is certain that whatever seeming calamity happens to you, if you thank and praise God for it, you turn it into a blessing.

Could you, therefore, work miracles, you could do no more for yourself than by his thankful Spirit; for it turns all it touches into happiness.

THIS WAS A TURNING POINT FOR ME

It may sound a bit simplistic, but a turning point in my life came when I read this, typed it on a card, hung it on my wall and thought about it each day for a year. It made me view my circumstances not as simply good or bad, but to view them as all good.

As I internalized that level of understanding, my mental paradigm began to grow. Try it yourself. Not just thinking it mentally—because this won't work—but actually by writing William Law's statement on a card and placing it where you can read it each day. And when you read . . . think! Do this repeatedly, day in and day out, for several months, and I promise you that something interesting will happen.

Choose a Success Environment

The third action guide was . . . Choose a success environment—select people, places, things that support the person you want to be.

I once interviewed a couple for a magazine article who'd achieved a level in a direct sales company that only five other people out of hundreds of thousands had achieved. Starting out as a math teacher in a small college earning less than eight thousand dollars a year, the man and his wife went on to earn over a half million dollars a year.

I asked them how they did it.

"Really pretty simple" was the reply. "When we started we'd pick out someone who was above us and we'd get to know them. We'd learn from them. We'd associate with them. We'd see the standard of living they enjoyed.

"Pretty soon," they explained, "we'd mysteriously be performing on the level they were. Then, we'd pick out someone else who was ahead of us, and we'd do the same thing." This went on and on until they gradually found themselves at the top.

Notice two things. They carefully set small short-term goals, and they quickly rose to conform to the environment they selected.

Now don't misunderstand, I'm not talking about coldly using people in order to climb past them. But it does show the power of our environment—the people, places, and things we choose to associate with.

SUMMING UP

Your mental paradigm is the imaginary boundary you place around yourself. Although it's below the conscious level, it's still well defined. Whatever it is, it controls all your actions, feelings, behavior, and abilities.

Rather than have this knowledge be frustrating and fatalistic, it can be exciting and life-expanding. It can, but it's your choice to make it that way. Your personal belief system has been formed by your reaction and perception to thousands of your life experiences. It can be changed only by consciously discovering the truth about yourself and structuring success experiences.

It won't be changed one iota by reading this book. It will change only when you first *decide* to change it and then apply the concepts of this book, when you set success goals and take action. All the abstract thinking in the world won't change it—it's changed only by positive action.

I gave you some positive action guides. Write them on a card and carry them all week. Memorize William Law's quotation. Read this chapter several times this next week. Look for and recognize success principles each time you read; don't just read for information. Doing this will involve your feelings and emotions and cause you to *experience* these concepts.

I know this about you: You have the ability to reach goals and enjoy whatever quality of life you desire. The quality of life you experience, though, is determined by your own beliefs. What you believe you *should* have and *can* have is what you *will* have. Nothing controls your quality of life as much as your own belief system—your mental paradigm— not circumstances, not education, not even your past.

Understanding this chapter will get you started in a positive direction. The rest of this book will give you specific direction.

3

Discovering Your
Goal-Seeking Mechanism

Ove Johansson came from Sweden to the United States to play soccer for a college in West Virginia. While working in Texas one summer, he helped organize a youth soccer league for the city of Irving. He met and soon married his wife, April, who was a student at Abilene Christian University, and he transferred there.

Late one November he attended a football game—which was his first. As a friend was explaining the game, he routinely explained that a field goal was where you kicked the ball through the uprights and got three points. Ove nodded and asked an obvious question. He asked, "Well, why don't they kick the ball more?"

His friend explained that in college football not many people could kick over thirty-five yards.

Not understanding this limitation, Ove said, "Oh, I could kick it much farther than that!"

His friend responded, "Then why don't you?"

To which Ove said, "Okay, I will!"

Without broadcasting it, he set a goal in his head to kick a football farther than anyone had ever done before—and to do it in one year. To this day, he still doesn't know why he set that goal or why he even believed he could accomplish it.

Beginning in January of the next year, he started practicing each afternoon in the cold west Texas weather. At first the ball didn't exactly cooperate because it wasn't the right shape—it wasn't round like a soccer ball. But he kept after it until he began to develop more accuracy.

His practice took on an interesting routine. He's not sure how or when he learned to do this, but he began to patiently program his Goal-Seeking Mechanism. Notice carefully what he did.

Each afternoon he'd go out to a practice field and begin kicking. At first he'd kick from the point where the end zone and sideline intersect. Now visualize this angle and how narrow an opening he had. Then he'd move the ball back to the ten-yard line and sideline and kick.

Gradually he'd move the ball farther and farther back—widening the window above the goalpost. Then he'd move the ball in to the hash marks, then to the center of the field.

From there he had what seemed to him an incredibly large opening above the goalpost—which he later said, "made it look like I had the whole world to kick through!"

HE LEARNED TO VISUALIZE HIS GOAL

He later explained to me that he played another interesting mental game. Before each kick he'd stand behind the ball and visualize two things:

1. his form in approaching the ball, and
2. the ball going perfectly between the uprights.

After visualizing what he wanted to happen, he'd then kick—forgetting any form but just doing it the way that felt most natural. He'd watch the ball, and regardless of where it landed, he'd mentally correct his kick. He'd visualize it going where he wanted it to go instead of where it had gone.

Then he'd walk and pick up the ball. When he picked it up, regardless of where it was, he'd stop, look back at the kicking tee and visualize himself kicking the ball. He'd mentally detail his approach and form. He'd "see" the ball leaving the tee and going perfectly between the goalposts. Then he'd walk back, tee the ball up, and begin the process again —for two to three hours each afternoon.

"Didn't that get boring?" I asked him.

"Never," he responded. "It was so exciting—I enjoyed hundreds of successes each afternoon!"

PERSISTENT PRACTICE PAID OFF

As the months passed, he progressed steadily and during the middle of the summer he was out one afternoon banging

50–60-yard field goals with ease. A young man who played tight end for Abilene Christian saw him and was aghast.

Approaching Ove, he asked, "Do you know what you're doing?"

"Ya," Ove responded, pretty low-keyed.

"Why, you're . . . you're kicking close to the world record!"

"Ya," Ove replied.

"How far can you kick?" the young man asked.

"Oh, sixty, seventy yards," Ove replied, "You want to see a good one?"

"Yeah!"

"Okay, watch this one!"

He teed the ball up and booted a sixty yarder with ease.

"Wow!"

"Let me show you another!"

He teed the ball up and banged one sixty-five yards.

"Want to see another one?"

"No, no . . . you . . . you just stay right here . . . I'm going to get the coach!"

So the player went screaming into the coach's office and yelled, out of breath, "Coach, coach . . . come out here . . . there's a guy out here kicking sixty–sixty-five-yard field goals!"

The coach almost went into cardiac arrest. He went running out to the practice field and met Ove.

"Let me see you kick," he said.

So Ove chipped a couple of fifty yarders for him.

"Want to see a long one?" Ove grinned.

"Yeah."

So he backed up and blasted one from way off—in a rush

of adrenaline, no one even remembers exactly how far it was.

Coach Wally Bullington signed him on the spot and gave him a half scholarship—which was all he had left to give.

THE SEASON BEGINS

In August I began a nine-week leadership training course for the team and met Ove for the first time. Immediately I could sense that he was someone special—a very gifted young man who contributed great things to our class of about twenty-five players.

He had an excellent season. In October, for a homecoming game with East Texas State University, he felt the time had come for him to reach his goal.

TIME FOR THE GOAL!

So the day before the game he and Wilbert Montgomery, who would later star for the Philadelphia Eagles, went into Coach Bullington's office and laid out their grand plan.

"Tomorrow, we're going to set *two* world records, Coach!" Ove announced.

"Wilbert is going to set a record for scoring more touchdowns in his collegiate career than anyone else has ever done!" (He lacked only one to surpass Lydell Mitchell's record set at Penn State.)

He went on. "And I'm going to kick a field goal farther than anyone has ever done in a game before!"

The coach grinned and told him that if he looked good in their pregame warm-ups, then he'd let him have a shot. Within a few minutes all the rest of the players knew about it. Adrenaline began to rush through their veins. No one slept all night.

I conducted pregame sessions and worked on the bench with the players during the game. I'd never seen such excitement. During warm-ups, Ove booted three seventy yarders. All the kids got pumped even higher, though the opposing team wasn't all that thrilled.

Then in the second quarter with fourth down on their own 41-yard line, the coach turned to Ove. All it took was a slight nod and he shot onto the field for a 69-yard attempt. The homecoming crowd went crazy—the opposing team looked a bit disoriented.

On the count, the center snapped the ball, the holder smoothly placed it on the tee, and in one swift, fluid motion, Ove's foot smacked the ball. It sounded like someone had scored a direct hit on an elephant's flanks with a high-powered rifle.

A NEW WORLD RECORD!

The ball went . . . and went . . . almost as if in suspended animation. Then suddenly, the official's arms shot up. A new world's record of 69 yards! The ball would have cleared 75 yards easily. Congratulations came in from all over the world. Reporters called Ove from dozens of newspapers and wire services.

After the dust settled, Ove and April were our houseguests for the Thanksgiving weekend. Late one evening we were talking, and he casually said to me, "Ron, I didn't kick that football with my foot!" He watched me carefully to see if I was really listening to him. "Oh," I replied.

"I Kicked the Football with My Head!"

"No, I kicked it with my head," he said, tapping his temple with his index finger. Then he told me again of his visualization and how he'd learned to program his mind and let it influence the physical action of his body.

Often, when I tell this story, people want to know what happened to Ove. He was injured during his last collegiate game. (He played only his senior year.) Drafted by the Houston Oilers, he wasn't rehabilitated by summer camp. Then Philadelphia brought him in to kick for two games, and he pulled a hamstring. The next summer Dallas brought him into training camp. He had the team made, but Rafael Septien came in with more experience.

Today Ove is very successful in the insurance business.

HOW YOUR GOAL-SEEKING MECHANISM WORKS

Now, why do I tell you Ove's story? Do I think you could go out and kick a record field goal? No, of course not! We all have our talents, gifts, and different possibilities. Ove found his. You have others. I have others. I tell the story to illustrate how your Goal-Seeking Mechanism works. Yes, *"yours!"*

What Ove has, you have—a brain, or mind, a Goal-Seeking Mechanism, that operates much like a modern computer to help us reach goals. All of us use this mechanism each day—but most people don't know they do. Every time we drink a cup of coffee or take a bite of food or comb our hair, we use this mechanism. It doesn't have to be used just for world records.

When we understand how the mechanism works, it opens

lots of doors of growth for us—large and small. When you learn to use it, you can weigh what you want to, earn what you want to, live in the kind of home you want to, enjoy the level of physical and emotional health you want to, or actualize the spiritual resources you want to.

When you learn to use this incredible power, you'll find many ways to use it—from simple habit changes to major life changes. Here's a simple way I recently used it to change a habit.

A few months ago I noticed that I walked with my right foot twisted to the right—like a duck. So I decided to program my computer to cause me to walk straight. I programmed my computer by saying around a hundred times a day, "Right toe, pigeon toe!" Whether this makes sense to you or not, it was my way of overcorrecting my foot.

I didn't consciously try to walk differently, I just gave myself this command a hundred times each day. I programmed my mental computer, and within thirty days I was unconsciously walking with my right foot straight. By programming my mental computer I had unconsciously straightened my foot. (I repeated the word *unconscious* for emphasis because that's the level on which all this happens.)

An insignificant example? Maybe, but it reveals the secret that's behind every discovery that man has made. Now, again, this experiment may sound pretty insignificant to you, but it was a profound learning experience for me. Although I already intellectually knew it would work, I'd never experienced it. So it was a new emotional learning experience.

On this subject, Dr. Maxwell Maltz wrote, "Every living thing has a built-in guidance system or goal-seeking device, put there by its Creator to help it achieve its goal—which is, in broad terms, to live."

He pointed out that animals "know" what to do at certain times. Squirrels "know" to store away food for the winter without ever having experienced the need before. Birds "know" to fly to certain places without any training. Fish "know" to swim up to where they were hatched without any education.

He also writes, "Man, on the other hand, has something animals haven't—Creative Imagination. Thus man of all creations is more than a creature, he is a creator. With his imagination he can formulate a variety of goals. Man alone can direct his Success Mechanism by the use of imagination, or imaging ability."

The truth is that every person has one of these Goal-Seeking Mechanisms. Each of us has this built-in mental computer.

MOST PEOPLE DON'T USE IT!

The problem, or tragedy, is that most people go through life *not knowing* they have one and *not using* the one they have!

And another fact is that those of us who know we have one don't always use it. I use mine to reach some goals, then struggle vainly to reach other goals—only to realize later that I haven't been doing what I know to do! I haven't been using this powerful inner resource that's been silently awaiting my asking for help.

Again, intellectually knowing this and knowing it from experience are vastly different. I've presented these concepts in seminars and workshops, only to have people come up to me at breaks and yawn that they've *heard* all this stuff before. Then when I ask them how they've put it into *practice,* I get blank stares.

My conclusion is that there are a lot of other people like me who may have heard of these concepts, but who don't always *practice* them. I say this, not knowing your level of awareness. So whether this is new and thrilling to you, or you're sophisticated and have heard all this before, let me clear the deck and gather us all at the same point.

Let's all admit that we're learners who know a little but not much—at least, not much compared with that giant universe of wisdom that our Creator exhibits in forming and maintaining this and the thousands of other galactic systems!

AN EXERCISE FOR DISCOVERING THE POWER OF YOUR THOUGHTS

Let me give you an exercise—a simple one that will help you better understand one dimension of your Goal-Seeking Mechanism.

First, select two or three friends who have approximately your own strength and have a fair degree of seriousness and ability to concentrate. Ask these people to stand up facing you, to raise one arm level with the floor and make a fist. Place your hand on their wrist and ask them to resist you as much as possible. Then test their strength for both of you to get an idea of what it is.

After this, ask them to lower their arms and just relax. Then ask them to close their eyes and visualize a negative, unhappy experience. To think of a time they were angry, hurt, or depressed. Ask them to recapture the experience and mentally dwell on it. Then ask them to shoot those negative feelings throughout their entire bodies.

Allow a half minute for them to concentrate on the negative experience, and again ask them to raise their arms, clench their fists, and resist you as much as possible. Then test their arm strength again, and be surprised to find they only have a small fraction of their previous resistance.

Ask them to explain how they felt. Let them explain. Then ask them to take a deep breath and just relax again. After a couple of deep breaths ask them to close their eyes again and this time to recall a very happy, positive experience that's recently happened to them. Ask them to visualize an actual experience when they felt good and were happy and confident.

Give them a half minute to internalize this experience— again sending these pleasant, happy, confident feelings throughout their bodies. Then ask them to raise their arms again, make a fist, and resist you as much as possible. What happens will startle them when they see how different they feel and how much more strength they have.

Try it. It'll almost always work. Why? Because our thoughts influence our physical strength. Positive thoughts, fed to our Goal-Seeking Mechanism, cause us to be strong. Negative thoughts make us weak. What we choose to think about influences us on many levels.

OUR GOAL-SEEKING MECHANISM HELPS US DEVELOP NEW HABITS

Years ago I learned to program my own mental computer, my Goal-Seeking Mechanism to help me stop smoking. I did it by saying to myself fifty times each morning and fifty times each afternoon, "I enjoy life without smoking!" I also began visualizing my lungs being coated with black, yucky tar each time I smoked a cigarette.

When I started this visualization and repeated these suggestions to myself, I also kept on smoking. The truth is you don't quit smoking by using logic or willpower. You quit by emotionally changing your belief system—by reprogramming your Goal-Seeking Mechanism, which we'll get into much deeper in later chapters.

At first, I felt a conflict because I still smoked while going through the programming. Then one day I was driving down the highway and impulsively reached for my pack of cigarettes and chucked them out of the car window. I questioned my sanity when about twenty miles later I gave in and stopped and bought another pack.

But I kept telling myself fifty times each morning and fifty times each afternoon, "I enjoy life without smoking," even though I kept on smoking.

The "chuck the pack out the window" routine happened two or three more times. I always felt guilty when my willpower didn't last long. But I kept up the self-suggestions and visualization.

Gradually cigarettes began to taste bad due to my visualizing the tar in my lungs, and then finally one day arrived when I threw them away, and I experienced a brand-new emotional sensation! I *emotionally* knew that this truly was *the* time. And it was!

Not because I'd used willpower. Because to use just willpower to change such a deeply engraved habit as smoking almost always ends in failure. It does because our emotions are much more powerful than willpower. William James, a philosopher and Harvard professor, said it eloquently almost a hundred years ago when he wrote, "When the will and the emotions are in conflict, the emotions almost always win!"

What a powerful bit of wisdom that is!

What I had done was to work on the cause level. I changed the way I *felt* about cigarettes, and then my behavior *automatically* changed. Understand this and you'll understand how habits are broken or why they're not broken.

Do you want to quit smoking? Lose weight? Break another habit? Develop a new one? You can best do it by learning about how your inner, emotional, Goal-Seeking Mechanism controls these habits.

One of the greatest needs we have is to develop new habits or break old ones. Seventy-five percent of the people who have been in goal-setting seminars I've conducted set goals to lose weight. I've written weight-management programs and have helped thousands of people to successfully lose weight and maintain their desired weight level. And the secret was that our programs got them first to set a specific weight goal—what they wanted to weigh the rest of their lives. Then we taught them how to program their mental computers, their Goal-Seeking Mechanisms, to silently steer them to their desired weight goal.

Here's the story of a real person who achieved her permanent slimness goal:

I've been on every diet there is. I've lost several hundred pounds—only to lose a few pounds by crash dieting, getting frustrated and ending up weighing more than I did when I started.

But your program helped me reach my goal of one hundred twenty pounds. I lost fifty pounds. And this time I know I'll keep it off. I will because I've changed the way I see me.

I did what you taught us to do. I first set my permanent slimness goal. I dug out a picture of me when I weighed one hundred twenty pounds and looked at it every day. I repeated to myself over and over, "I weigh one hundred twenty pounds!" I went out and bought a new dress that would fit me when I reached my goal. I hung it up in my dressing room and looked at it each day —visualizing myself wearing it by my target date . . .

I didn't try to deprive myself of food, I just kept programming my mind to really believe that I weighed one hundred twenty pounds . . .

I reached my goal and I feel terrific. But I'm more excited about the fact that I now know how to reach whatever goals I want to reach—by changing the way I think.

What a great example! Study it and you'll discover the success principle that's embodied in these three thoughts:

1. You have a powerful inner Goal-Striving Mechanism—a mental computer.
2. You can consciously set goals and program them into this computer.
3. This mechanism then takes over and unconsciously helps you reach the goals.

I have repeated this several times for emphasis.

You'll have a lot of questions about how this mechanism works. I still have lots of unanswered questions. No one really knows how it works—just that it *does* work. And maybe that's all we really need to know.

How? Well, as I just said, that's what most of the rest of this book is about—helping you program your Goal-Seeking Mechanism so you can reach goals that are important to you.

AN ACTIVITY TO HELP YOU DISCOVER YOUR GOAL-SEEKING MECHANISM

Here's a simple, quick activity, in addition to the ones I just mentioned, that will help you discover how this powerful inner computer works. Try this exercise tonight just for fun.

1. Two or three hours after dinner one evening, think what snacks you have in your pantry.
2. Settle on one that seems most appealing.
3. Then visualize how it would taste. If it's salty, visualize how great it would taste. If it's sugary, visualize how great the sweet taste would be.
4. For five minutes, try to think of nothing but how wonderful that snack would be. Think about the taste, the satisfaction of chewing and swallowing.
5. Then after five minutes, do whatever you feel like doing!

Give this a try and see what happens. Then analyze your response. Could you resist the urge to go get the snack? Probably not! If you mentally enjoyed thinking about the snack, you were strongly motivated to get up and actually enjoy it. Your visualizing the snack programmed your Goal-Seeking Mechanism, which then took over and delivered the goal of satisfaction.

Now I'm not trying to put pounds on you, just trying to help you learn a profound concept in a simple way. Incidentally, if you want to *quit* nighttime snacks, start programming your mind to *not* enjoy them. Visualize them having germs on them or being dirty or rotten. Keep this programming up and you'll come to not want them.

CONSCIOUSLY SET GOALS
AND YOUR GOAL-SEEKING MECHANISM
UNCONSCIOUSLY HELPS YOU REACH THEM

Our minds are so complex that they encompass both the conscious and unconscious parts of us. With our conscious minds, we use logic, learn, and think. But the unconscious part of us is the dynamic, creative part that directs us to our goals. Without evaluating whether our goals are right or wrong, this inner Goal-Seeking Mechanism goes to work to being into reality the goals that the conscious mind sets.

Your mental computer doesn't evaluate what your goals should be—that's for your value-driven conscious mind to do. Scanning your desires, ambitions, beliefs, and values, your conscious mind determines and selects the goals that are important and meaningful for you. It sets them. Then your unconscious mechanism, without questioning the rightness or wrongness of those goals selected, silently goes to work to help you reach them.

You can observe this in many of your daily activities. Have you ever been preoccupied and lost in thought while driving to work? You got to work, but you didn't consciously notice a thing on route. What happened was your unconscious mechanism directed you until your goal was reached. Now this doesn't sound too profound, but when you experience it and then analyze it, it's almost miraculous.

Another way to observe your unconscious silently at work is through your hunches and intuition. Ever wrestle with a problem to no avail, only to wake up at 3 A.M. with the solution clearly in focus? This happens all the time—because our inner guidance systems are silently at work within us, steering us to our goals.

When you begin to learn this concept, you'll see how your unconscious Goal-Seeking Mechanism works in many ways. You'll then be excited to know that you can direct it and let it help you reach any goal that's important to you.

SUMMING UP

You have a built-in guidance system, a Goal-Seeking Mechanism, given to you by your Creator to help you reach goals that are important to you. This chapter has been designed to get you to think about this—how it works in simple ways and how it might work in more complex ways.

Most people live and die and never discover this inner computer. Most people never learn how to use it, so their lives are controlled by circumstances, happenstances, or by ups and downs.

This inner mechanism is so powerful that it can help you reach any kind of goal you want to reach—either positive or negative. It's up to you to choose! You can choose to use this mechanism to help you reach creative, productive goals. This is one of man's greatest discoveries.

The reality is that each of us has to discover this for ourselves—usually over and over, on different levels. You can discover this Goal-Seeking Mechanism and you can also get good at using it. You can . . . when you assimilate and apply the principles of this book.

The next chapter gets you setting specific goals. The following ones will then tell you how to make them become realities.

Part II

If one advances confidently in the direction of his dreams, and endeavors to live the life which he has imagined, he will meet with success unexpected in common hours.

—HENRY DAVID THOREAU

4

Setting Meaningful Goals

In the late 1920s, after twenty years of practical research with the most successful people in our country, Napoleon Hill produced his first great work, *The Law of Success.* In it he wrote this about the power of goal setting: "Any definite chief aim that is deliberately fixed in the mind and held there, with determination to realize it, finally saturates the entire subconscious mind until it automatically influences the physical action of the body toward the attainment of that purpose."

Napoleon Hill captures many powerful insights in that one sentence. It really sums up the first three chapters of this book.

As you've read the first three chapters of this book, you've been exposed to many powerful, profound thoughts. Here are a few of the points I've made:

1. Each of us has a powerful inner belief system, formed by our reaction to all our life experiences.
2. This belief system influences all our actions, feelings, behavior, and abilities.
3. As we expand this belief system, our actions, feelings, behavior, and abilities *automatically* expand.
4. We each also have an inner Goal-Seeking Mechanism that can help us reach new goals—when we know how to use it.

These thoughts in the first three chapters are sufficient to help you grasp the power we all have at our disposal. They can help you prepare for greater goal achievement. I repeat —they can help you prepare for greater goal achievement.

So let's get into action! Let's get on with a process that will help you bring exciting new levels of achievement into your life!

A GOAL ACHIEVEMENT SYSTEM

The following Goal Achievement System is a step-by-step process, which, when followed, will help you define and reach specific goals. As I've written before—this process isn't something you *intellectually learn*. Rather it's something you *emotionally experience*. There's a big difference.

The Goal Achievement System has five parts. They are

1. setting goals,
2. planning strategy,
3. building belief,
4. developing strengths, and
5. evaluating progress

I've put this into a simple, logical, easy-to-understand order so that, rather than experiencing goal setting as a hit-or-miss, stab-in-the-dark system, you'll learn a workable process.

Analyze almost any goal you've ever set and reached and you'll discover that you either consciously or unconsciously followed these steps.

My grandson, Brian, just learned to ride his bicycle without training wheels. If I were to dissect his learning experience, we'd see that he pretty much followed these five steps.

A friend in the life insurance business picked me up for lunch last week and told me that he'd reached a major goal and that in the last month alone he had earned $30,000 in commissions.

I asked him how he did it, and guess what? He had followed my Goal Achievement System pretty much to the letter.

Here's a diagram of the system.

GOAL ACHIEVEMENT SYSTEM

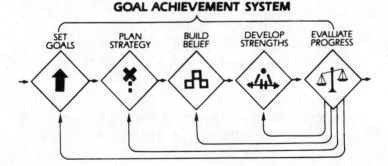

Look at the preceding illustration again. Take a few minutes and study it. You'll be struck with the simplicity and uniqueness of it. In this system I've brought all the elements of goal achievement together. All you have to do is add the ingredients of desire and action in order to make it work for you.

I challenge you to prove me right or wrong—with your actions.

GETTING INTO ACTION

Well, until you take action and implement my system, you'll never know whether it'll work for you or not. So . . . let's get into action!

In order to get into action, I want you to get a pad of paper and a pen or pencil. Please read the following questions and write responses to the ones that are meaningful to you. Okay, no cheating now! Don't just read these and mentally answer or just think about them. Get a pen and paper and write your responses!

Here's the list of questions. Please read each one and write your response to the ones that suggest a desirable response. Some will be meaningful and appropriate; others won't be. Skip over the ones that aren't.

1. How much would you like to weigh?
2. How much money would you like to earn next month or next year?
3. What specific habit would you like to develop?
4. What specific habit would you like to break?
5. What personality trait would you like to develop?
6. What kind of home would you like to own?

7. What improvement would you like to make in your present home?
8. What would you like to do on your next vacation?
9. How would you like to communicate with family members?
10. How would you like to communicate with co-workers?
11. What new office would you like to enjoy?
12. What new position would you like to attain?
13. What new honor would you like to attain?
14. What specific person would you like to have as a closer friend?
15. What improvement in your physical condition would you like to make?
16. What professional or occupational skill would you like to strengthen?
17. What artistic or creative talent would you like to develop?
18. What kind of person would you like to marry?
19. What new hobby would you like to begin?
20. What new activity would you like to begin?
21. What one thing could you do to add more enjoyment to your life?
22. What one goal could you reach that would solve a specific problem you now have?
23. What one goal could you reach that would lessen tension or stress in your life?
24. What one activity could you do that would relieve pressure or worry?
25. What study habits would you like to acquire?
26. What grade-point average would you like to earn?
27. What additional education would you like to have?

28. What physical activity would you like to start?
29. How much money would you like to save each pay period?
30. What specific financial habit would you like to develop?
31. What debts would you like to pay off?
32. How much each month would you like to have when you retire?
33. How much money would you like to leave your family in case of unexpected death?
34. What charitable contributions would you like to make?
35. How much merchandise, goods, or services would you like to sell? ach month, quarter, year?
36. What specific sales skills would you like to strengthen?
37. What would you like to do for your church?
38. What would you like to do for your community?
39. What civic interest or public service would you like to be involved in?
40. How would you like others to describe you?
41. What image would you like to communicate to others?
42. What specific actions can you take to build up your family members?
43. What family activities can you start doing?
44. What common interests can you plan to involve yourself with other family members?
45. What spiritual goals would you like to reach?
46. What spiritual qualities would you like to develop?
47. When people describe you, what three words would you like them to use?
48. What other things would you like to have happen to you in the next year?

Well, these are a lot of questions, and they require some decisions. This is a very important step. Now that you've written answers to the ones that are meaningful to you, here's what I want you to do.

Step 1. Please go back and review your written responses to the questions again. Reflect and think about your answers. Then select six of them as your most important ones. Place a check mark by each of the six.

If you have a difficult time making decisions, here's a simple way to do it. Look over all your responses and select the one *most*-important goal. Check it. Then the *next* most-important . . . and so on.

Step 2. When you've selected the six most-important ones, look at each one and put a time limit or date of attainment beside it. Write down the date when you want to achieve the goal.

When doing this, give yourself plenty of time to achieve your goals. Don't be unrealistic. Nothing happens overnight —although many of your goals will come into reality before you expect them to do so. But for now, be realistic about your target dates.

Step 3. When you've written target dates beside each of your goals, then comes a most important step. Now you're going to write your goals into definite statements. When you do this, please follow this suggestion. Write them like this:

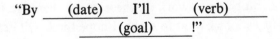

Let me give you some examples.

"By May 15 I'll weigh one hundred eighty pounds!"
"By July 31 I'll average sales of two hundred thousand dollars' worth of life insurance each month!"

"Beginning January 1, I'll save ten percent of my income each month!"

"By the end of this next semester I'll have a 3.0 grade-point average!"

You get the message, don't you? Write your six goals into a definite statement and put a time limit on each one—write them the way I've suggested. Why? I'll fully explain it in a later chapter. The main reason is that it puts your goal in the form of an active self-suggestion.

Step 4. Now, when you have all six goals written like this, get six 3 × 5 index cards. On each card, write one goal statement on one side. Write them in exciting colors— maybe each in a different color. After writing them on the cards, put a rubber band around them. You're going to carry the cards with you and read them each day.

YOU'VE TAKEN THE FIRST STEP

Congratulations! You've just done something that very, very few people have ever done. You've set some specific, meaningful goals. There's more to the process than just writing our goals, but you've taken the first step.

As you apply the suggestions of the next four chapters, you'll begin to reach the goals that are really important to you. As you begin to work on these goals, there are two or three suggestions I want to make. I hope these will help you while you work to achieve your goals.

First, let me say that these goals aren't cast in bronze or etched in marble. They can be changed. If you read them a week from now and one doesn't seem nearly as important as it did when you set it, change it. And if your target date appears to be a bit unrealistic, change it. Or if you discover a month from now that one goal conflicts with other goals, change it.

Changing, or refining, goals can show progress—if, of course, you're not just being wishy-washy and weakly committed to them. The level of your commitment is another vital consideration.

YOUR GOALS SHOULD BE CONSISTENT

Goals in conflict can create problems. To prevent this, look at your goals again, and then answer the following questions.

1. Are your goals consistent with your other goals?
2. Are they consistent with your spouse's goals?
3. Are they consistent with any of your values?
4. Are they consistent with other peoples' goals with whom you have to work?

As I said, these are important questions to ask yourself. Many people undermine themselves because their goals are in conflict or aren't consistent with the areas I've just mentioned. Tensions and self-defeating pressures are set up that make the process unpleasant rather than exhilarating.

YOUR GOALS SHOULD BE STATEMENTS OF THE DESIRED END RESULT

Many people say they set goals, but upon analysis what they call goals are only vague wishes or hopes.

I've asked many people if they set goals, and they'd reply, "Sure!"

When I ask what goals they set, I get less than specific responses. Like, "My goal is to lose some weight!" Or "My goal is to get a better job!" Or "My goal is to make more money." Or "My goal is to get a larger home."

Examine all these responses and you'll see a common problem. None are specific. They contain words like "more, better, good, some, larger." These words keep their statements from being specific goal statements.

So please watch out for these and other words that keep your goal statements from being specific. Analyze each of the preceding responses and you'll see that none states a specific end result. And that's what a goal is. Stated in the most simple terms that I know—*a goal is a statement of the desired end result!*

In the goal-setting seminars that I conduct, I always get around to this simple, basic concept. I start participants from ground zero by having them write down this statement. "A goal is a statement of the desired end result!"

Sounds pretty elementary, doesn't it? In a sense, it is, but the problem is that most people don't understand this.

GET READY FOR AN EXCITING EXPERIENCE

Now that you've written your goals on the six index cards —assuming that they're specific and meaningful for you— get ready for some exciting things to happen.

Occasionally I dig out old goal-setting booklets in which I set goals several years ago. It's fascinating to go back and reread them and see how many actually happened. I'm always amazed at how many actually came into reality.

As I've looked back at these over several years' time, I've noticed some very common patterns. Here they are

1. A high percentage of the goals were accomplished.
2. My income goals were almost never reached on schedule—but they were almost always reached a year later.
3. My goals evolved from year to year—reflecting my changing mental paradigm.

Looking back can be an exciting experience. It also helps build belief in the Goal-Achievement System.

SUMMING UP

In this chapter I presented to you my five-part Goal-Achievement System. Then you took pencil to paper and did the first part—you set some goals. You did something that few people in the world have ever done before. What an exciting step!

You also learned how to make sure your goals are specific and not vague and too general. You learned that a goal is a statement of the desired end result.

Please carry your goal cards with you and read them each day. Spend the next week scanning this chapter several times. If you need to change or revise your goals, do it. That shows progress.

In the next chapter, you'll learn how to plan your strategy for reaching these goals. Then, in later chapters, you'll learn to build belief and develop strengths. These will help bring your goals into reality.

I'm excited about sharing this system with you. I know from many years of experience what can happen when you follow it correctly. I'm excited about the lifelong *resource* the system can be for you.

My enthusiasm isn't just for the goals you've just set;

rather it's for the <u>fact you now have a system to use</u> for the rest of your life. It's like the old saying, "Give a man a fish and he'll eat for a day. Teach him *how* to fish and he'll eat for life!"

I hope my system teaches you "how to fish" and that it contributes to your prosperity for the rest of your life. It will . . . when you follow my instructions and work the system precisely as I present it to you.

5

Planning Strategy
for Reaching Your Goals

As a high school student, Kelly Forehand had a goal to be a
stockbroker. But during his senior year something happened that appeared to curtail his goal achievement for the
rest of his life. In a high school football game, he was hit
from behind and knocked to the ground. This had happened
many times before, but this time his spinal cord was sev-
ered. Lying on the ground, unable to move or breathe, he
thought his life was all over. An emergency unit got him

breathing again, but he would live the rest of his life a para-plegic.

Kelly then entered extensive therapy and was given an electric wheelchair and van that he could drive. He entered college and graduated with a BBA degree in management and a minor in finance. He still had his goal of being a stockbroker. He wanted to work for Merrill Lynch. There was a problem, though. They wouldn't give him a job be-cause of his handicap, although the manager's excuse was that he was too young. But that didn't deter him. He kept believing and planning for the day he'd get a job as a broker.

After several months of not finding a job, he came to work in our office doing telephone sales. He was up front and honestly told me that his ultimate goal was to be with a brokerage firm. I encouraged him to keep the goal and at the same time to learn as much as he could about sales.

He kept his goal in mind and continued to prepare him-self, believing that his chance would come. He read business magazines, the *Wall Street Journal* and other publications. He developed work habits and discipline. He kept in contact with a Merrill Lynch broker. He took two courses in invest-ments, taught by an ex-stockbroker. His chance eventually came—as he knew it would. Four years later a new manager came to the local office and Kelly interviewed with him and got a job. In the ensuing years, he's been successful, produc-tive, and fulfilled.

His is a great example of setting a goal and then carefully planning his strategy, believing that at the right time the goal would be reached. He kept doing everything he knew to do to prepare himself for the goal.

The second step of our Goal-Achievement System is planning strategy. Sometimes our strategy can be carefully planned; at other times we have to spend time discovering the strategy.

TWO KINDS OF GOALS

There are basically two kinds of goals:

1. Where the strategy or steps of achievement are known, they just have to be taken.
2. Where the strategy or steps are unknown, they have to be discovered.

For some goals, such as building a home, it's pretty simple to plan your strategy. You simply hire a builder or an architect to design a plan—a step-by-step process of constructing a home. Then execute the steps of the plan. But for goals that don't exist yet—like getting a better job or developing a spiritual value—it's often difficult to plan our strategy.

And there are still other factors that influence our ability to plan our goal strategy. Here's an important one: Planning is a left-brain logical exercise that requires that we have fairly good concrete organizational ability. But setting goals is usually a right-brain activity—dreaming, believing, and visualizing goal attainment. Often these two dimensions aren't both actualized in the same person.

My experience has been that people who can get emotionally charged about enjoying new goals often have problems laying out clear plans. I've also observed that few people will actually sit down, on their own initiative, and map out a goal strategy. And then another interesting observation I've made is that those left-brain, detail-minded people who do plot out elaborate goal plans often get their enjoyment from *designing* the plan, whereas *working out* the plan somehow falls through the cracks.

ALL YOU NEED TO KNOW ABOUT PLANNING

In the last chapter, you learned to define goals. You learned how to write them into a definite statement and put a target date on them.

Let's assume that your target dates are usually pretty realistic—although it's often hard to know what's realistic and what isn't.

Here are four simple questions you can ask that will help you get your planning job done.

1. What's my target date to reach this goal?
2. How can I break my goal down into subgoals or incremental steps?
3. What activities will it take to complete each incremental step?
4. What activities can I perform today?

Go back and read these four steps again, and you'll see that they'll get you a long way down the road in goal planning. They address both the long and short terms. They also bring the reality of goal achievement down to today.

It's easy to fantasize about reaching distant goals and never bring the responsibility for achieving them down to today. But to be successful the pressure to reach goals should be a daily one, not a distant one.

Jack Fuqua is a good friend, who has been successful in the life insurance business for more than thirty years now. He consistently places in the Top of the Table, an elite group of around three hundred Top Million-Dollar Round Table members.

I remember him saying something over twenty years ago that at first sounded like a cliché. After digging deeper into what he said, I learned a great lesson in goal planning.

I asked him how come he was so successful; his reply was, "Oh, I just plan my work . . . and then work my plan!" I'd heard that bromide spouted trillions of times before, but it became fresh and alive after he explained what he did.

Jack opened his pocket planner and showed me how he set an annual goal of life insurance premiums. He broke it down into monthly amounts—allowing for seasonal fluctuations. As I recall, he took the past three years' monthly and annual sales and averaged what percentage of the year's sales occurred during specific months.

He then projected that same monthly percentage for the coming year. So, instead of just taking one-twelfth of his annual goal for each month, he made a more educated guess, which allowed for season fluctuations. He then looked at what his closing averages had been on qualified calls and what his average sale was.

With these basic assumptions based on experience, he used them as projecting and planning tools. This was how he planned his strategy for achieving his new sales goals. He projected for each day, week, and month the prospects or referrals he'd need. He knew he'd have to see a certain number of prospects to make one sale. He also knew how many sales he'd have to make to reach his goal.

I was impressed with two things. One, the fact that he took time to plan his work so carefully; and two, that he saw *action* as being the most important ingredient. His strategy was pretty simple, but it worked for him. It worked because he was also committed to action—to work his plan. He had a bias for action.

Study his planning, and you'll see some ideas that you can use in your own goal planning. He had a specific long-term goal. He broke it down into incremental steps or subgoals. He then outlined what activities he'd need to perform. Then he committed himself to daily action.

BREAKING YOUR GOALS DOWN INTO INCREMENTAL STEPS

In 1961 President Kennedy set a goal to have a man go to the moon and return by the end of the decade. At the time it sounded impossible. Who really believed it could be done? But the president was serious. So a team of scientists was formed to develop the strategy.

The rest is history. That may have been the most difficult goal that I've seen set and achieved in my lifetime—an incredible event! You've read about how they did it. Basically, they identified each incremental step they'd have to take, and they developed a strategy for each step. Then, eight years later, the goal was reached.

How can you break down your goals into subgoals, or incremental steps? Your goal may be to earn a certain sum of money, or to retire, or to have a specific net worth. Or it may be to run a marathon or a ten-kilometer race. Or it may be to get a higher degree of education or to lose twenty-five pounds.

Many of our goals can be broken down into steps, or subgoals.

It's a good exercise to stop and see how many subgoals

you can structure so that when you've reached every small goal you automatically reach your main one.

OFTEN YOU CAN'T PLAN OUT YOUR GOAL ACHIEVEMENT

There are some goals that you can't sit down and lay out a plan for achieving. The reason you can't plan them out is that they come as the result of a creative idea. You must have "light bulb" experiences for these goals to happen.

In other words, your unconscious works together with your experience, knowledge, and inner beliefs and . . . zap . . . you wake up in the middle of the night and the way to reach your goal is apparent.

Your answer, or creative idea, didn't pop into your consciousness because you laid out logical, concrete plans but, rather, because another dimension inside you was also working on the problem, or goal. This gives birth to hunches, flashes of insight, creative discoveries. All of us use this dimension. Many people, such as Thomas Edison, Albert Einstein, Werner von Braun, who are thought to be creative geniuses, use it to a fine-tuned degree.

All of us use it in simple, everyday ways too. Each time that I've written a book or a training course I have to select a title. Usually the title isn't selected until after the book is fully written.

My goal is always the same—to select a title that has some excitement and either arouses interest or tells what the book is about. Usually I'll spend many hours, over a two- or three-month period of time, brainstorming ideas. I'll write down as many as I can think of, without attempting to come to a decision.

Always, the same thing happens. I get frustrated because I can't come up with just the right one. Then, just when there seems to be no hope, the right title pops into my mind. It pops into my mind at the strangest moments—at 3 A.M., or while I'm swimming, or while my mind is charged up doing a seminar, and other times. In each case, my Goal-Seeking Mechanism steers me to the achievement of the goal.

Mike Ritt, who handled all of Napoleon Hill's work when he was managed by W. Clement Stone, told me this example of how Hill got the title idea for his famous book, *Think and Grow Rich.*

Mr. Hill had written the book and had given it some crazy-sounding title; the publisher hated it. He pressed Hill for a better, more zingy one. Still, nothing. Finally, he told Hill that they had to go to press the next day and that if he didn't have an acceptable title that he would name it himself.

"What will you call it?" Hill asked.

"We'll call it *Use Your Noodle to Get the Boodle!*"

Hill screamed his displeasure, "That's awful. It'll ruin the book and me!"

The publisher stood his ground and said, "Well, you get me a better one tomorrow, or that's it!"

This put the pressure on Hill. "Tomorrow, I've got to have the title tomorrow!"

His mind went to spinning. *"Use Your Noodle to Get the Boodle* is terrible!"* he repeated to himself over and over. He could hardly go to sleep. Then he slept fitfully, tossing and turning.

Then, whap! In the middle of the night he sat up in his bed as if someone had set off a charge of dynamite.

"That's it!" he exclaimed. "That's it! *Think and Grow Rich!*"

He called his publisher immediately, woke him up, and laid this great title on him. And the rest is history. Millions of copies were sold. Probably more people have been motivated to higher success because of that one book than any other one besides the Bible.

SUDDENLY THE ANSWER APPEARS

You've experienced the same sensation—times when you set a goal that you didn't know how to achieve. You kept the goal in mind and thought about how to achieve it. Then suddenly, out of nowhere, the answer came.

We got our present home the same way—as the result of a creative idea. About twelve years ago, we decided that we wanted to get a new home. Our daughters had both gone off to college, and our needs had changed. So we set a goal to get a new home.

But my goal was somewhat restricted by these conditions: one, that I'd pay at least two-thirds of it in cash; and two, that I wouldn't take the money out of my business. Now, since my business was my only apparent way of making money, that really put the pinch on me.

I began to follow the Goal Achievement System. I mentally pictured the goal and the amount of money it would take. I selected the home and drove past it each day. I did other belief-building activities each day . . . and guess what? Nothing happened! I couldn't figure out how to get the money. Nothing happened the first month, nothing happened the second, third, fourth, fifth . . . nothing happened. But I kept visualizing the goal.

Then, one day out of the clear blue sky, something happened. It was the answer to the question, "How can I get the money?" It was the plan! All neatly laid out in front of me in a sudden flash of creative thought.

I'll never forget it. I was conducting a three-day seminar in Los Angeles. One morning, after breakfast, going from the first to the fifth floor, it all hit me—like a bolt out of the blue. The answer! How I could get the money!

It had taken six months of programming my mental computer for it to spit out the plan, the answer, or the solution —*which had been there all along, awaiting my discovery!* It was very simple. My creative mechanism had finally put the right combination together.

I had written some self-concept programs for an educational company to market to public schools. In lieu of royalties, I received 25 percent of the company stock. Since the balance of the stock was wholly owned by the president, I had no control of it. I received no dividends and had no real say in the management.

The president had grandiose plans for the company, but I seriously doubted his ability to make them happen.

That evening I called him and for thirty to forty-five minutes he extolled his own abilities and built these huge air castles of wealth that we were going to have soon.

"I know you have high confidence in your abilities to make a lot of money," I told him. "And . . . if it's going to be made, it'll be done by you. . . . Realizing this, you should enjoy most of the rewards. . . . How would you like to trade me this other stock you own [I mentioned the company] for your stock that I own—that way you'll own a hundred percent of your own company."

He liked the idea. As soon as I got the stock from him, I

sold it for what was then a very substantial sum—enough to buy our current home.

Now, what's my point?

It's this. Most of our goals can be reached only by creatively discovering the "how to" of "means whereby." This may be a combination of ideas that together form the solution or strategy.

THE ROLE OF OUR CREATIVE IMAGINATION

It's here that our own creative imagination plays a big role in bringing these ideas, discoveries, or insights into combination. Many people of high achievement aren't any smarter or luckier than others, it's just that they've learned how to program their creative mechanisms to work for them.

Scotty Witt is a good friend, who, almost thirty years ago, came out of the army with a very strong goal. It was to build a youth camp in the mountains for young people to enjoy during the summers. An outdoorsman, he had worked at a camp one summer in New York while in the service.

When he came back to our city and announced his goal, everyone thought he was having a grandiose dream that would soon pass. But it didn't. In a few months, he found a dude ranch in northern New Mexico that was for sale. He scraped together a small down payment and had six months to make a larger one. He worked night and day, getting almost nowhere. No one wanted to give him money for a scheme that probably wouldn't work.

In the frustration of weeks of butting his head against a stone wall, a creative idea suddenly came to him. The idea was to sell cabin sites to people to finance the purchase of the ranch. He immediately staked out lots and found significant interest in them. This creative idea helped him get the necessary funds to complete the second payment.

You, too, have had creative ideas that helped you reach a goal. Everyone has—because that's how our minds work. But successful people have learned how to *cause* this creative mechanism to work more efficiently for them. They've learned how to program their mental computers to help them reach their goals.

You can, too, when you apply the concepts of the Goal Achievement System.

Often you can't plan for a goal because you don't know what to do to make it happen. So you have to keep programing your inner goal-Seeking Mechanism, believing that it will help you discover your plan.

This is one of the miracles of creative thinking . . . and of goal achievement.

A BIAS FOR ACTION

Tom Peters, in his book *A Passion for Excellence*, written with Nancy Austin, refers to successful companies as being ones that have a "bias for action."

That's rather cleverly said and also right on target. Most successful people I know have a "bias for action." They see *action* as being the important step in goal achievement.

Unfortunately, many other people have a "bias for dreaming" or a "bias for planning." All that many people do is talk or dream. Still others lay out elaborate plans. Then often the plans become the objective, rather than the objective being the objective.

Several years ago I was a classic example of planning being the objective rather than goal achievement being the objective. Our firm had been doing job skills training for the Department of labor and affiliated regional councils of government. We assessed and trained unemployed people to have better interviewing and job skills. Our training focused on increasing the self-esteem of unemployed people, getting them to set goals, and building belief that they could reach them. We had some incredible results with hundreds of people who'd given up on themselves.

When I called on the director of one of the regional planning councils, I immediately noticed that charts and graphs completely covered his office walls. I'd never seen anything like it before. You couldn't find a square inch of blank wall space between all his elaborate charts and graphs.

The moment I met him he told me how very busy he was and how he didn't have much time to talk because he had so much to do and had such a tight schedule to do it on. He was very closed and defensive when he thought I was there to sell him something. He kept telling me how busy he was and trying to brush me off, and why he *didn't* need any training programs.

But when I asked about his charts, I noticed that he had plenty of time to explain to me his long-range planning strategy as well as how he organized his own time and managed it so well. The whole time was spent with him talking about how busy he was planning everything.

I also quickly got the message that he had no time to talk about either implementation or results. And, of course, he was far too busy to entertain any new ideas. Any time I suggested how we had helped other agencies, his response was, "We're much more highly organized than they are, and what you're suggesting wouldn't fit into our long-range plans!"

It was sad, but it was also funny how he had no openness for anything that smacked of action. It was also interesting how nothing active in nature "fit into his long-range plans."

You've also seen people who spend their time organizing rather than doing. There needs to be a balance.

An interesting contrast to this kind of person is my neighbor, Boone Pickens. Few people, in the last five years, haven't heard the name of T. Boone Pickens, Jr. "Oilman," "corporate raider," "opportunist," "respected businessman," are some of the labels that have been hung on him.

But whatever label that's hung on him usually misses the point of his example. The real message is what can happen to a person who is sharp, bright, has a high achievement drive, and is willing to go for seemingly impossible goals. Starting with a few thousand dollars of borrowed capital, he built his company to the point that one year he was the highest paid CEO in corporate America.

In conversation recently, he revealed part of the mind-set that was the *source* of the wealth. The discussion centered on how his small company was able to be so nimble, yet highly aggressive—to do things that companies many times their size couldn't do.

He briefly explained their decision-making style. He said that their executives look at every opportunity, its pros and cons, and once they have all the facts and information, they make a quick decision. He went on to emphasize that once a decision has been made, they then get into action. They lay out plans and carefully begin to execute them.

In his attempts to take over major oil companies, he had strategies and alternate strategies. But the exciting part of his success was his ability to change plans and to react to roadblocks and apparent dead-ends. In his book, *Boone,* he details some of the hair-trigger moments he encountered in some of his negotiations.

Pickens definitely has "a bias for action."

SUMMING UP

This second step of our Goal Achievement System is about planning strategy for reaching your goals. We thought about two types of planning:

1. concrete planning that we can logically do; and
2. discovering the steps or strategy through creative imagination.

I suggested that there are some goals that can be planned out in a concrete, organized, logical way. There are others for which the means of achievement have to be discovered by creative imagination.

I mentioned these four questions that will help get you started on planning strategy for some of your goals.

1. What's my target date to reach my goal?
2. How can I break it down into subgoals, or incremental steps?
3. What activities will it take to complete each step?
4. What activities can I accomplish today?

These questions, asked and answered daily, can help you plan your goal strategy.

I mentioned the importance of action. Planning without action can be a substitute for success for non-risk takers.

Action without planning can be "Ready, fire, aim." It takes both, in the right order.

Please spend this week reviewing the goals you set last week. Read this chapter once a day. As you look at your goals, take some time, and as best you can, plan your strategy for reaching them. Get a loose-leaf notebook and write each goal at the top of a page. Then make notes on the page of how you can reach the goal. Write action ideas. Let that be your strategy page. If you can break them into subgoals, do that and then plan the strategy for reaching each small goal.

Each day answer this question: What can I do today to reach my goals? As you get answers, take action and do the activities that you need to do. As you absorb this message, by reading it each day for a week, you'll especially prepare yourself for the next chapter—the most important one.

It's the most important one because it gets at the real essence of failure or success in goal setting. It teaches you the most important step in the Goal Achievement System. But before you go to it, be sure to write out your strategy for achieving your goals.

6

Building Belief in Your Goals

Several years ago, our firm conducted about twenty-five three-day Psycho-Cybernetics seminars for the Illinois Division of Vocational Rehabilitation. We trained unemployed handicapped people to get jobs and keep them.

We saw what appeared to be miracles happen to many of the people. Let me tell you how a couple of people's lives changed. See if you can pinpoint *why* they changed.

The first seminar was conducted at the University of Chicago, where about seventy-five handicapped people had been enrolled by their caseworkers or counselors. Most of the people were from south Chicago, and as they came in the first morning, it looked like a death march. No enthusiasm, no excitement, no life. We had paraplegics, quadriplegics, blind people, deaf people, amputees—all kinds of disabilities.

As the participants were filing in, I began to feel depressed. Suddenly, I lost my usual preseminar "up." I began the session by reaching down into my reserve and pulling up as much emotional energy as I could. As I looked into a sea of dead faces, I connected with one that was bright, smiling, and giving me massive nods of approval. So I focused in on him.

At the first break, I found out that his name was Henry Mortensen. Henry was in a wheelchair, looked to be around thirty years old, and had one of the brightest smiles I'd ever seen. I found out that day that he'd never had a job and had been on welfare for several years.

I'd never seen anyone more positive or anyone who threw themselves into a seminar more than Henry did.

The first day we gave them some assessment instruments and tried to get them to identify some of their strengths. The second day everyone set goals, and the third day they developed plans to reach their goals. Laced throughout the three days were team-building exercises, along with lots of discussion and interaction at their tables.

In the three days, the whole group, seated eight to a table, just came alive. Skeptical at first, they soon accepted the idea that I was sincerely interested in them. When this happened, they dropped their defenses and really got into the flow of things.

Several of them kept in touch for a few years afterward. I got letters telling of weight loss, new jobs, and things for their homes. Gloria Collier wrote me each Christmas for several years. She'd gone to school and become a nurse.

About a year after the seminar I got a letter from Henry Mortensen. He began his letter by saying, "You probably don't remember me, but. . . ."

He was wrong. How could I have forgotten him? He went on telling me that he'd set three goals during the seminar. They were

1. to get a business of his own,
2. to earn over nine thousand dollars the first year, and
3. to get married.

He continued: "If you'll look at this letterhead, you'll see that I've accomplished my first goal."

I looked at the letterhead, which read, "Sales on Wheels . . . Henry Mortensen, President."

Henry explained that he'd gotten a motorized wheelchair and was selling home-care products door to door. He then proudly told me that he had exceeded his second goal— which was to earn nine thousand dollars the first year.

And then he must have had a smile on his face as he finished his letter. "As for my third goal . . ." he went on to explain it. He wrote that he'd gone out and enrolled in a dance club for handicapped people, met a young woman, and they were soon to be married.

What a story! I read and reread the letter many times that day. Over and over. Asking myself the same question. The question that I'll ask you. It's this: Considering the fact that the handicap that had caused him to be unemployed and on welfare hadn't changed at all . . . but his whole life had changed . . . the question I kept asking myself was, "What was it about Henry that changed?"

What was it? You're right! The only thing that changed about him was his *beliefs!* His attitude! His mental paradigm. Nothing else had changed—except, of course, his whole life!

Now, before we go on, would you please stop reading for a few moments and ask yourself, "What does this mean to me?" How does this principle apply to you? It does, you know. It does to all of us. The fact that Henry was handicapped has nothing to do with the lesson to be learned. My point is that he learned to improve on his condition—a condition that he had mentally accepted before.

We're all guilty of accepting certain standards and conditions of life. Many of us suffer mental paralysis. We allow our belief systems to dictate our achievement. We often accept limitations without challenging them.

Sometime later I conducted another seminar for handicapped people down in Joliet, Illinois. Again, we had about seventy-five people in attendance. Seated at one of the front tables were eight men, all in wheelchairs. As we began, I noticed that one of them was accompanied by his wife, who was helping him communicate with the other people at his table.

The man had a post coming up from the right arm of his wheelchair, and he rested his right wrist on a pad on top of the post. He made no attempt to talk to the other men at his table. He'd utter some seemingly inaudible words to his wife, who'd then translate them to the other table members. Occasionally, she'd stick a yellow tablet in front of his hand, and he'd scribble some words on it for her to read and interpret. That's how he communicated most of the first two days.

During a break the first day I found out that his name was Bob Brinkman, that he'd been in an automobile accident ten years before and had been temporarily paralyzed. His wife explained that for a year he went to therapy, but he had quit going. She told me that he wouldn't go out of their home, that he'd just sit in his wheelchair, not wanting to see anyone or go anywhere.

She explained that the doctors had released him, saying there wasn't any more they could do for him—that he could walk if he wanted to. Then she looked at me with heavy, hopeless eyes and said the saddest thing I'd ever heard. She said, "But he doesn't want to!"

Once I walked by his table and heard another man say, "Bob, if there was any chance in the world that I could walk . . . I'd at least try!" I wanted to go out into the hall and cry. It was so sad.

We ended each day of the seminar by having each table vote for one person who'd gained the most from the day's session, and we presented them with a self-help book award.

I'd go around to each table and have the discussion leader stand and announce the winner's name. The winner would accept the book award, and I'd stick the microphone up to his or her mouth and ask how it felt to be a winner.

In time we got around to Bob's table. His table leader announced into the microphone that their winner was . . . Bob Brinkman. The whole group applauded wildly. Without thinking, I stuck the microphone in front of Bob and asked, "Bob, how does it make you feel to be a winner?"

Suddenly it dawned on me what I'd done . . . that he couldn't talk. "What do I do now?" I panicked.

What happened next shocked me. In the press of emotions, Bob began to talk. You couldn't understand him very well, at least at first. But he kept talking. I tried to find a way to gracefully let him off the hook, but it became quite obvious that he wanted to talk. So I let him go. He must have talked for ten to fifteen minutes.

He began very slowly and haltingly. He hardly made sense. But then his speech began to clear up. After two or three minutes, you could understand him quite easily. It was like a blossom opening up and giving birth to a beautiful new flower.

He told the people about his accident, about his temporary paralysis, about his fear. Then he told them of his new goal—to walk again. Again, everyone applauded. I can't remember what else he said, I was so caught up with emotion.

About a week to ten days later, I got a letter from Bob. Opening it, I saw that he'd written on one side of the page, and his wife had written on the other side. I suppose she thought I might not be able to read his writing.

His letter began by saying that two or three days after the seminar he asked his wife to take the children and leave for two hours—that he was going to walk, and he wanted to do it himself. She did.

Bob told of wheeling himself over to the stairs in their home and sitting there for what seemed like an eternity—attempting to summon up the courage to walk up the eleven steps. He mentioned the fear. His muscles had become weak. He was suddenly afraid of falling. Then, he said, he got up and, one by one, managed to climb the steps—all eleven. He told what a victory it was.

I read the letter over and over that morning, lost in my

own emotions and searching questions. "What had happened that made Bob admit his fears and take action to overcome them? . . . I wonder what will happen to him now?"

Then my thoughts turned from Bob to myself. "What fears do I have that I haven't faced yet? What kind of mental wheelchair do I have me in? What kind of 'steps' could I climb if only I could put off my self-imposed limitations?" The questions went on most of that day. I am still asking myself those questions.

Now, you might be saying, "Why are you telling these two stories? Most of your readers aren't physically handicapped." Of course, I agree. But my overwhelming belief is that most of us *are* handicapped! We're locked into small paradigms. We're handicapped by our fears, self-imposed limitations, and belief systems.

Most of us have no idea of the power we have, or the heights we could climb—if we could only believe. Jesus Christ, speaking with the wisdom of the Creator, said, "If you can believe, all things are possible for him who believes." Believing . . . what a profoundly interesting concept!

WHAT IT MEANS TO BELIEVE

I've used the word *believe* many times in this book. Maybe we should stop and define it. To do so, let's first isolate two kinds of belief—intellectual and emotional.

Intellectual belief is a passive acceptance or understanding of facts, information, or knowledge. I believe the earth is round and is approximately twenty-five thousand miles in circumference. I believe in the law of gravity. I believe we won our independence from the British. I believe that two plus two equals four. These are intellectual beliefs.

Emotional beliefs are different. I believe that my wife and children love me. I believe that I can touch audiences. I believe that a Divine Creator loves and accepts me. I believe I should weigh one hundred ninety pounds. I believe that I can earn a certain income range. I believe that I should enjoy a high level of prosperity. These are emotional beliefs. They're inner, unconscious beliefs that guide and control all my actions, feelings, behavior, and abilities.

As I've written earlier, this inner, unconscious belief system dictates the level of my accomplishments. It silently defines the parameters of my achievement. I can't act or perform in a manner inconsistent with this central belief system.

My major point is this: *None of us can achieve goals until we expand our own inner belief systems to fit the size of the goals we set.* Understand that, and not only will you know something that most people don't know, but you'll also understand why goals are achieved and why they're not achieved.

But all of this is mere philosophy until you *experience* it, and this is a self-help *action* book. I'm not as interested in being philosophical as in helping you make something happen in your life. So, let's get to the most important part of this chapter and think about exactly *how* you can expand your own inner belief system to fit the size of your goals.

HOW TO EXPAND YOUR OWN INNER BELIEF SYSTEM

Here are four practical ways you can expand your belief system. When you practice these specific activities, you'll begin to see yourself differently:

1. affirmations,
2. visualization,
3. graphic representation, and
4. environmental influences.

Let's take each of these actions and think about it for a few minutes. Then I'll close this chapter by summarizing how you can systematically use all of them.

AFFIRMATIONS

Affirmations are words we say to ourselves. They're verbal suggestions we say silently or out loud.

The truth is that if I tell myself something often enough and long enough, I'll eventually believe it.

Affirmations, suggestions, or self-talk is a very common activity. It's also very subtle in helping shape our lives. We do it each day whether we're aware of it or not.

"I just can't lose weight!" "Everything I eat turns to fat!" "I'm just not good at math!" "I'm not athletically inclined!" "I'm not a creative person!" "Things like this are always happening to me!" "Why did I do that?"

These and thousands of other common statements we feed ourselves form our self-talk. And guess what? If we persist in them, we'll eventually come to accept them as truth—to believe them or emotionally accept them as fact. This principle works on the deepest, most profound level of our existence.

Let me give you a common example. Several years ago, I lost about thirty pounds. For some time I'd weighed between 215 and 218 pounds. One day I stepped on the scales and the figure had moved to 220.

"That's it," I said to myself, "I'm going to lose some weight." For several years prior to that, I'd been on all sorts of diets—water diets, grapefruit diets—all kinds. The results were predictably the same. I'd lose five or six pounds, feel starved, get off the diet, gain the pounds back, and feel like a failure.

It dawned on me one day that I wasn't practicing what I preached. I'd never first changed my inner picture of myself; and until that changed, nothing else would.

So I took out a 3 × 5 index card and wrote on it, "I weigh 190 pounds." I put the card in my pocket and began carrying it each day. I began saying the affirmation 50 times each morning and 50 times each evening. Sometimes I'd say it out loud, and sometimes I'd say it silently. At first I felt strange doing this, but I persisted. In addition to these daily affirmations, I added another dimension to my programming. I began a daily visualization exercise.

VISUALIZATION

One way I did this was to take a twenty-minute relaxation period each day—listening to a relaxation tape I'd written and produced. The tape had soft music and directions on how to go into deep relaxation.

Once into the relaxed state I'd mentally see myself weighing 190 pounds. I'd see how trim I was. Then I replayed the same scene each day. I'd visualize myself going into a men's clothing store and selecting a slim-cut suit, trying it on in front of a four-way mirror, noticing how trim it looked.

I played this same scene each day, along with repeating my affirmations. In about three weeks, I began to notice subtle changes in my appetite and in the portions of food I ate. I noticed that I just didn't want as much food as I had previously. It wasn't that I was using discipline, it was simply that I wasn't as hungry as before. I also noticed that I could leave food on my plate—for the first time in my life.

I learned that you don't lose weight by willpower. Willpower only compounds the problem—it makes us more aware of food and eating. We lose weight by first changing our desires and appetites.

The reality was that as I focused on my goal of 190 pounds, my inner creative mechanism began to work out the way to reach the goal. And that's what happened. In three months I weighed 190 pounds and have maintained that weight for over ten years now.

I used affirmations and visualization to program my Goal-Seeking Mechanism—my inner computer that is so powerful that it controls my pulse rate, metabolism, lymphatic flow, and all of the other physical and mental functions. I worked on the cause and then the effect took place.

Successful athletes have known this for years. Over the years I've heard many professional athletes tell about using this creative power of visualization to enhance their performance.

George Brett, the great baseball player of Kansas City, once told in an interview how he did so well. At the time he was batting an unbelievable .400. The reporter asked him how he did it.

Brett told of going to bed the evening before a game, closing his eyes and seeing himself hitting singles, doubles, and home runs. He'd see his bat connect with each pitch that was thrown. He'd visualize the baseball being as big as a basketball. He'd imagine the balls coming so slow that he could see the stitches on them.

He'd learned to use visualization to help build belief. He understood that his belief *would then* be translated into physical action. While he didn't sustain this .400 batting average for the rest of his career, this technique of mental rehearsal no doubt has had a big part in his outstanding career.

In a recent *American Way* article a reporter interviewed diving great Greg Louganis. The article told how he employed as much mental preparation as physical training. It went on to say:

His mental preparation entails the practice of visualization, in which he actually "sees" himself performing a dive before he ever goes off the board. Of this practice, Louganis says:

"In the last few years it's become a real popular topic with all of the sports psychologists, telling athletes that they should envision themselves doing certain things before they ever do them. But I was really amazed when it all started because I'd been doing it for years and was pretty surprised to realize that everybody else didn't already do it too.

"Whether I was singing or dancing or diving, I've been doing mental rehearsals since I was three years old. Through any given competition, I will do a dive about ninety times in my head before I ever get on the board, and I'll do it to music. Then, when I am on the board, I just relax and stop thinking about anything, and at that point the dive becomes a reflex."

Well, you may say, "But I'm not a professional baseball player or an Olympic diver." And I understand. But my point is that you don't have to be. You can learn and practice the same principles in your own life—regardless of where or who you are.

You can practice these principles in two ways:

1. by visualizing yourself performing the activities that are required for you to reach your goals;
2. by visualizing yourself *already* enjoying your goals.

If you wrote out your goals as I directed in Chapter 4, you'll see that they're actually stated as affirmations—designed for you to say to yourself several times each day.

GRAPHIC REPRESENTATION

The third way to build belief in your goals is to use graphic representation.

What is graphic representation? It's looking at pictures, words, slogans, symbols that remind you of your goal.

Almost twenty years ago I began conducting a leadership course for a college football team. In it, we talked about goal setting, and I suggested that the team members might like to cut out a picture of a player they'd like to be like.

One of the most outstanding examples of character and commitment I've ever seen was packaged inside a kid named Pat Holder. Pat was all of about five feet six inches tall—if you stretched him. He played wide receiver. He was slow and short, but he had a massive desire to win.

He took my advice seriously and cut out a picture of Lance Alworth, at the time a star wide receiver for the San Diego Chargers. He hung the picture on the wall near his bunk, and he would lay down, relax, and look at it each day, each time visualizing himself playing as well as Alworth. He'd also visualize himself being ten feet tall.

He kept doing this programming, and his play became outstanding. Many times I saw him go up between two defenders who were well over six feet tall and come down with the ball. A five-foot six-inch person can't outjump a six-foot person, but he did consistently.

That year in a pretty tough conference, as only a sophomore, Pat made first team all-conference. He caught passes all over the field.

In the same class was another young man who had all kinds of athletic ability but wasn't using it. He was a senior and wasn't expecting much of himself. He'd never delivered much either.

This young man's name was Bob Oliver, and near the end of his last season he really came alive. By a quirk of fate, Blanton Collier, then coach of the Cleveland Browns, saw Bob on film one day. Actually the coach was watching the film of a running back they were interested in drafting, but the problem was that the back kept getting tackled by some unknown defensive end named Bob Oliver.

The coach called Bob and asked him if he'd like to try out for them. Bob was speechless. He asked me what he could do to prepare himself to make the team, and I suggested several goal-setting techniques. One was to cut out a picture of Bill Glass, who was an all-pro defensive end for Cleveland but was retiring.

Bob did this and told himself that he was going to have

Glass's job. Then, to make a long story short, here's a part of a letter I received from Bob the next September.

Dear Mr. Willingham,

I have made the top forty players of the Cleveland Browns. I would like to thank you for helping me accomplish this goal.

I came into camp with the attitude that nobody would out-hustle me and that I would learn my position quicker than anyone else on the team.

I want to thank you for helping me accomplish my goals.

Bob played for the Browns for two years before suffering a knee injury that forced him to quit. Just making the team was a tremendous achievement for him. He did it by mentally picturing his desired performance.

Thousands of people have been through a weight-management course I wrote for the Shaklee Corporation. The unique factor of the program was that it was a method of changing a person's internal belief about what they "should" weigh.

One technique we used was to have the people make goal posters. These were collages, which, at the top, had a picture of the people taken at a time when they weighed their ideal weight. If they didn't have one, we had them glue their face on a magazine picture of a slim body.

Then on the goal poster were words, slogans, and pictures that supported their slimness. They cut out pictures of foods they'd eat. They glued pictures of clothes or other rewards they'd give themselves when they reached their goals.

This graphic representation helped many build belief and shed the necessary pounds to achieve their weight goals.

The power of visually looking at their goal posters helped influence their inner belief systems.

ENVIRONMENTAL INFLUENCES

The fourth way to build belief in your goals is to structure supportive environmental influences. Our environment—people, places, things—influences our success. We'll usually conform to our environment. It has a powerful influence on us. We'll become like it.

In this regard, here are some miscellaneous suggestions that will help you structure supportive environmental influences:

1. Carefully choose the people with whom you associate. Choose people who are performing or living on the level you'd like to perform or live.
2. Choose a growth environment where you can learn, grow, and have unlimited opportunities.
3. Associate with people who have common values and achievement drives as you.
4. Expose yourself to other people's prosperity:
   a. drive through wealthy neighborhoods,
   b. read biographies about successes, and
   c. visit stores where wealthy people buy things.

Wealth is first a state of mind, then it translates itself into reality. These environmental influences can help develop greater prosperity consciousness.

I love to drive through Beverly Hills and look at the homes. When I first began to do this years ago, they were totally outside my own belief system. But to drive through these neighborhoods and to go into the shops tells me that a lot of people have mentally accepted that level of prosperity. That means it's possible. And if it's possible for them, it's possible for me too. This experience always has a very positive influence on my own belief system.

The big question for you, then, is, "How can you structure environmental influences that will expand your own belief system—your mental paradigm?"

SUMMING UP

In this chapter I've said that before you can reach a goal you must first build belief in it—you must accept its existence as a reality. All of your goals will carefully elude you until your belief is built.

I gave you four ideas—four ways to build belief in your goals. They were

1. affirmations,
2. visualization,
3. graphic representation, and
4. environmental influences

There are two keys to making these four suggestions work for you:

1. repetition—doing these action guides each day, over and over; and
2. time lapse—consistently practicing the action guides daily over a period of time.

Since belief is an emotional process rather than an intellectual one, time lapse is necessary. It takes a minimum of twenty-one days of consistent practice to begin to change belief. It make take more. So, keep at it! Practice these action guides with repetition and time lapse. As you persist, you'll begin to feel changes in your own belief system.

Remember . . . any goal that's worthwhile is worth working for. Also, remember this principle: Before your goals can come into existence, you must first emotionally accept their reality—you must believe.

Faithfully practice the ideas in this chapter, and you'll begin to experience some thrilling, exhilarating new goals.

7

Developing Strengths to Reach Your Goals

One of my best friends, Bill Hale, is an ear, nose and throat surgeon who has a strong goal to help as many people as possible. Hundreds of people hear better today because of his expertise. Many people live through malignancies after he does surgical procedures on them.

Since his goal is to use his own abilities to help people, he's always learning and developing new skills—even after thirty years of practice. He knows that the success of his practice depends on staying updated on new procedures, techniques, and methods of treatment.

As I'm writing this book, he's doing a new procedure. He's implanting a tiny hearing device underneath the skin on a patient's skull. The device is screwed on to the skull. His goal is to help the patient hear better. To accomplish this goal, he had to develop some new strengths. He had to become certified to do the procedure. In doing this, he's following a very simple, although complex, Goal Achievement System.

Another friend, Dee Osborne, recently told me of beginning a copper-mining operation in Oman. His goal was to profitably mine copper and sell it for a profit. In order to achieve this goal, he had to learn about laws governing commerce in Oman. He found out that this previously backward country had no laws along this line. So he helped them draft new ones. He also helped them build roads. The development of this specialized knowledge was necessary for him and his partners to reach their goal.

A young man I know had a high desire to earn a place on his high school basketball team. His main weakness was that he was too short to get up into the air with the taller players. But, because of his strong desire, he began to develop his jumping skills. He practiced with ankle weights on. This began to build up his muscles so he had more spring in his legs. He made the team.

A friend who owns a builder's supply firm recently set a goal to manage his business more efficiently and get better management information. In order to reach this goal, he realized that he had to have greater knowledge of computers. So he enrolled in a course at a local college.

Basically, all of these people did the same thing. They all

identified a desirable goal and then asked themselves: "What will I have to do to reach this goal?"

WHAT WILL I HAVE TO DO TO REACH THIS GOAL?

Often, before a goal can be reached, we have to develop some personal strengths. And the same is true for even corporate or organizational goals. Developing strengths is part of paying the price to reach goals.

In conducting goal achievement seminars over the years, I've asked participants to assess the strengths it will take for them to reach their goals.

Here are four kinds of strengths you may have to develop in order to reach your goals:

1. attitudes,
2. habits,
3. skills, and
4. specialized knowledge.

Let's think about these individually.

ATTITUDES

An attitude is the way we think—about ourselves, about things, about others. It's a mind-set, a belief system, a viewpoint.

I've trained several thousand people to train salespeople to sell. Few things are more paradoxical than training, motivating, or managing salespeople. Some salespeople have incredibly high sales ability, but they don't sell. Others, seemingly, have few natural skills, but they sell. This paradox has driven many sales managers up the wall.

In recent years, we've been able to trace this paradox to one very important area: a salesperson's *attitude* toward selling. We find these attitudes among many salespeople:

1. They don't value the role of a salesperson; they don't feel good about being described that way.
2. They see selling as manipulation and don't feel good about it because it conflicts with their values.
3. They don't like the uncertainty involved.
4. They have a high fear of rejection.
5. They don't want to undergo the discipline and hard work necessary to succeed.

Basically, what we've found is that many salespeople have the wrong attitude toward selling; they view it as a process of doing something *to* people. We've discovered that when we can get them to see it as a process of *creating value* for people, their attitude toward it changes.

I've seen many salespeople set sales or income goals and not be able to reach them until they changed their attitudes toward selling.

Now, I realize that you may not be a salesperson, but look at the principle involved—*our attitude toward something influences our ability to perform.* It applies to all of us. Weak or negative attitudes toward ourselves, toward others, or toward things can block our goal achievement. I see it all of the time in people I train. I look back and see it in myself.

I recently bumped into a young man who had been in a training course I conducted more than ten years ago. He's since become very successful, and both he and his wife have been conducting seminars on a national level. His wife recently received the national honor of Policewoman of the Year.

The story began when I was to conduct a nine-week DynaGroup program for local police officers. In a precourse conference with the chief, he described several of the people. Half of the class was made up of rookie officers just out of school; the other half were seasoned veterans, some of whom had become discipline problems.

The chief reached over into his letter tray and opened up a file and began to tell me about Larry Bosch. He told me that Larry had been suspended three times for violent behavior and was now up for termination. He said he was withholding his signature pending the outcome of the course I was about to begin.

"He's really a good kid," the chief explained, "but just has never had a chance."

He then explained Larry's past as an abandoned child, growing up in a series of foster homes and finally ending up at Boys' Ranch, a ranch for delinquent, abandoned, or problem boys.

The next week the course began. I greeted the officers as they came in. Most were in uniform with name tags on their shirt pockets. In the stream of them, I spotted this good-looking, young, blond guy whose name tag said, "Bosch."

Reaching my hand out, I greeted him. When I did, he looked up at me and snarled some string of profane words and walked on past me. His message was quite clear. "I may have to be here, but I don't have to like it!"

During the first session, he sat slumped over, arms folded, seething. As soon as the session ended, *zip,* he was gone. The next week began as a repeat of the first session. He was furious about having to be there.

In the second session, each person was asked to stand,

take two and a half minutes, and tell about an incident from their life. Larry wouldn't have any part of that.

At the break, I went up behind him and attempted some communication with him. I touched him on the shoulder from behind, and he spun around as if I'd stuck a knife in him. He crouched, and I thought he was going to pull his gun or attack me.

I was kind of stunned and didn't know what to say, so I said something pretty stupid, like, "Well, how are you doing today, Larry?"

He looked at me incredulously and sneered, "Huh?"

"How are you doing?" I repeated.

"Well, what do you expect from a [blankety-blank, blankety-blank]!" he replied with utter contempt.

The blanks had to do with his mother's honor and his own legitimacy . . . and, oh yes, with certain condemning acts of God.

"What are you talking about?" I asked, not knowing what else to say.

"Well, no one has ever expected anything but bad from me, and I don't disappoint 'em!" was his reply.

Then he just unloaded. He told me of growing up in Michigan, being sent from home to home, being in street gangs, getting into all kinds of trouble, hating everyone, hating himself. . . .

He talked for several minutes, until it was time to get the session started again. Not wanting to interrupt him, I asked him, "Larry, I'm writing a program for preteen children. I'll bet you have some experiences that would help me. Would you mind coming by my office this next week and visiting with me?"

Now this was a street-smart young man. At first, he eyed

me skeptically and then, a moment later, said, "Sure, I'll come by."

I must say that I didn't really expect him to come by. But surprise of surprises! A couple of days later, my secretary announced over the intercom, "Larry Bosch is here to see you."

He came in and sat down on my sofa. My secretary brought in a pot of coffee and two cups. I asked him two or three questions, and he talked for an hour and a half. I mean—nonstop. I listened and made notes.

One question was, "Larry, if you had a chance to say something to thousands of kids . . . based on what you've learned from life . . . what would it be?"

As I sat back and listened, I was stunned at what I heard. He sounded like a Ph.D. social worker. He had some very good thoughts and some very mature insights. I saw very quickly that he was one intelligent young man.

At the end of an hour and a half he told me that it was time for his shift to start but that he'd like to come back. I told him how much I appreciated his taking his time, that he'd given me some great ideas. He left.

In the hour and a half that I had listened to him I witnessed something near a rebirth. A different person left my office than had come in. From a cynical, suspicious, hard person I saw emerge an intelligent, aware person filled with very mature insights.

What had caused this change in attitude? Who can really explain? Was it that I listened to him? That I showed I cared? That I said to him, "You're *worth* listening to?" No explanation sounds as profound as the experience was.

Then when the third session of our course rolled around, he was one of the first to show up. Positive, friendly, he visited with me and my course assistants. The change of attitude was unbelievable. He finished the course and made phenomenal strides of growth.

One week before the course ended, the chief called me and said, "I don't know what's happening to Bosch, but I'm tearing up his termination papers and giving him a promotion." Wow!

After that, Larry came by our office frequently just to visit. About two or three months after the course was over, I picked up the newspaper one morning, opened it up, and read this headline: LOCAL OFFICER SAVES MAN'S LIFE.

The front-page story began by saying that Patrolman Larry Bosch was driving down the street, spotted a man lying on the sidewalk, stopped his patrol car, and discovered that the man had died. The man's body was still warm, but he had no pulse.

Larry immediately radioed for an emergency unit and gave the man CPR; in a few seconds he had the man breathing again. The emergency unit arrived, and the man was taken to the hospital, where he spent the night. The next day he was released. Apparently, there was an electrical problem with the man's heart and it just stopped beating. Once it was going, he was all right. Shivers went up and down my back when I read that newspaper article.

A lot of great things happened to Larry after that. He got a bachelor's degree, began conducting seminars with his wife on rape prevention, and got a new job. He reached many new goals—goals he could only have reached with a different *attitude.* No longer was he fighting himself and the world for what it had done to him. He was a totally new person, ready to reach new goals.

And we're all this way! What new attitudes or ways of

thinking will you have to develop in order to reach your goals? What negative ones will have to become positive? How differently will you have to look at yourself, at the world, at other people? As you ask and get answers to these questions, you would do well to write them down.

I must warn you that this exercise in self-examination can be painful at times because our egos and emotional sets often feel discomfort when questioned or threatened. But this is necessary to help us reach new goals. Old, unchanged attitudes often block our enjoyment of new goals.

HABITS

A habit is an automatic response I perform, something I do unconsciously, instinctively, without thinking. I always put my right shoe on first. I brush my teeth the same way each day. I have to have a cup of coffee the moment I get to the office in the morning. I go to the YMCA and swim at 11 A.M. I drive to work the same route each morning. I go to sleep after watching only fifteen minutes of "The Tonight Show."

I'm a creature of habit. We all are. Some of my habits are good; others aren't so good. My good habits pay off for me; my bad ones keep me from enjoying the level of success I'm capable of enjoying.

Most successful people I know are successful because they've developed habits that produce positive results. I belong to the National Speakers Association, an association of professional speakers and trainers. At one of our conventions there'll be around a thousand people in attendance. You won't see a handful of them smoking. Very few are overweight or drink excessively.

The reason is that in order to survive the grind of speaking and training you have to have a high degree of stamina. We have to be in good health and focus massive amounts of physical and emotional energy on our appearances. And we can't do it without being in top physical shape. And we can't be in top physical shape when we smoke, drink excessively, or carry around too much weight.

For many years I did full-day seminars in cities like New York, Philadelphia, Detroit, and Minneapolis all in one week. The next week I might be in Los Angeles, Anaheim, San Francisco, and Seattle. I'd get to the meeting room at 7 A.M., set up, finish at 5 P.M., pack up, catch a plane to the next city, check into a hotel and get ready to do the same thing the next day. I'd give everything I had all day, knowing I had to do the same thing the next day and the day after.

My main goal was to be able to perform in a professional manner each day. So I developed eating, sleeping, exercise habits to help me reach my goals. I'd get nine to ten hours of sleep each evening after having a light dinner usually of fish or chicken. Twice each day I took Shaklee food supplements, along with instant protein. I ate high-fiber breakfasts with fruit. I drank lots of water during the day. I usually took a ten-minute nap at lunch before checking out of my hotel room. These healthful habits kept me in top shape and able to perform.

We're all creatures of habit. Habits influence our actions. Good habits guide our success. Bad habits can block our success. It's cause and effect. To a large degree, our success or lack of it is the result of our habits.

I was first challenged by this concept when I read my first self-help book, *Success Through a Positive Mental Attitude* by W. Clement Stone and Napoleon Hill. And then, years later, when I had the privilege of working with Mr. Stone, I understood more about the power of our habits in influencing our success.

Mr. Stone has a simple philosophy: If you want to be successful, you must first develop the habits that will cause success and break those habits that block success.

Most successful people have developed good time-management habits. Procrastination, indecisiveness, and inaction are weak habits that can be changed.

In reading *Success Through a Positive Mental Attitude,* I was forced to confront my habit of procrastination. Stone and Hill gave a solution. I tried it and it worked. They recommended memorizing the self-suggestion "Do It Now," to say the words over and over until they become permanently imprinted on our minds. Then whenever we see something that needs to be done, we can flash this mental command, "Do It Now," to ourselves.

I added another suggestion: "When I see something that needs to be done, I do it!" Then I repeated this to myself fifty times each morning and fifty times each afternoon. After this repetitive programming, every time I saw something that needed to be done, this command would flash into my conscious mind: "When I see something that needs to be done, I do it!" I would then follow through with action. That's how I developed a habit.

How Habits Are Formed

All of our habits are formed the same way! Habits are formed by consciously practicing certain actions repetitively, over a period of time. It takes *practice* and *time lapse* for them to be formed. It usually takes a minimum of twenty-one days of practicing an action before a habit can be formed.

Habits are broken the same way they're formed. They're broken by substituting another action or response—with time lapse and repetition.

I broke the cigarette smoking habit the same way I developed it. I developed it by making myself smoke until I got the hang of it. For weeks I'd smoke and cough, wheeze, sputter, and gasp. But with time and repetition I finally got the hang of it. I learned. I could then inhale smoke without dying. What a thrill!

Years later, I broke the habit by practicing other actions when I wanted a cigarette, instead of smoking—like deep breathing, or chewing gum, or eating (which wasn't the best way, because I gained thirty-five pounds in six months). I broke the smoking habit by replacing it with other activities until other habit patterns were established.

Habits are formed or broken by consciously practicing certain actions repetitively over a period of time. That's important to know.

What habits will it take to reach your goals? What habits will you have to break? What will you replace them with? As you review your goals, ask yourself these questions and record your responses. Doing this can open the doors to your new goals—or not doing it might keep the doors of your new goals permanently closed!

SKILLS

Skills are developed abilities. Reading, writing, and arithmetic are skills. Playing golf, painting a picture, sewing a button on a shirt. Performing a root canal, laser surgery to remove a cataract, a heart bypass, riding a bicycle. These are all skills.

In order to reach your goals, you'll probably have to develop some specific skills. Regardless of whether your goal is to be a legal secretary, accountant, computer programmer, or auto technician, you'll need skills.

A good question, then, is "What skills will you have to develop in order to reach your goals?" The skills that you define will then become subgoals.

Several years ago, a friend, who was also our family dentist, decided he wanted to move into the specialty of endodontics—the skill of saving teeth, usually by performing root canals. There were obvious skills he'd have to develop in order to become certified in that specialty. His next concern was, "How can I develop these skills?"

He had a family, financial obligations, and a general dentistry practice, so going back to school didn't appear to be an acceptable option. He then discovered that he could go into the navy at officer level, get all of the training he needed, and earn a high income, too. This solved his problem, or, rather, this was the way he could develop the skills to reach his goal of becoming an endodontist,

As it turned out, he loved the navy, had a lot of fun moving to different cities, and stayed in until he could retire.

Almost any goal takes certain skills. A friend of mine, Nido Qubein, is one of the top professional speakers in the country. Hear him speak and it looks so easy to do. He has excellent presentation skills, audience rapport, and command of words. He appears to be a born speaker. But that isn't the case at all!

Nido came to the United States from Jordan in his early

twenties, unable to speak the English language but with a burning desire to succeed. He enrolled in a college. He found it difficult to communicate. People used strange words that didn't make a bit of sense, descriptions like "cool" and "far out" left him scratching his head. Hamburgers had no ham in them; hot dogs had no dogs in them and weren't even always hot.

But he paid the price to develop his English skills. He studied, learned, and drilled himself. He stayed up late at night dictating words into a tape recorder and then carefully listening back to them. This practice and feedback helped him develop the ability to pronounce words and communicate. He also developed a lot of humorous material out of his learning.

Burning desire and high achievement drive made the effort worthwhile for him. Because of his strong need for achievement, he was willing to pay the price of hard work and effort in developing new skills.

What skills will you need to develop in order to reach your goals? As you ask this question of yourself (and, more importantly, as you get answers), you'll discover some important factors in reaching your goals.

SPECIALIZED KNOWLEDGE

The fourth strength you'll have to develop in order to reach your goals is specialized knowledge.

As our society becomes more technologically complex, this factor becomes more important. Today, for instance, automobiles have highly advanced technology. All of the gadgets and improvements on them make them very complicated to maintain and repair. Automotive technicians, who several years ago weren't thought of as being highly specialized people, today are. The specialized knowledge they need is very complex.

Computers, office machines, and modern electronics offer challenges to all of us. Most jobs today demand some knowledge of computers. I went into a business just last week to get a plumbing part. The clerk, who probably wasn't earning much above minimum wage, had to use a computer to check the inventory and then print out an invoice for me. All that took specialized knowledge.

Many goals demand specialized knowledge. How about yours? What specialized knowledge will reaching your goals demand?

Again, it will be helpful for you to write this down. Then if you're serious about reaching your goals, you'll begin to gain the specialized knowledge you'll need.

SUMMING UP

Well, no one said it was easy to reach goals. No one said it's effortless. And there's a price to pay for goal achievement. The price is often hard work and discipline. Often, people just aren't willing to pay those prices—which, of course, is okay because we all live in a free country.

Part of goal achievement is developing necessary strengths to reach your goals. We discussed those in this chapter. They are

1. attitudes,
2. habits,
3. skills, and
4. specialized knowledge.

What ran through your mind as you read this chapter? But, more importantly, what action did you take? What action do you plan to take? What price are you willing to pay to reach your goals? What will throw you off track and frustrate your goal progress and cause you to accept a mediocrity that puts no demands on you? These are penetrating, probing questions, but they're ones that need to be asked.

Are you willing to take the time to ask yourself all the questions that I've asked you in this chapter? And to write down your answers? Then take action? Are you willing to outline the attitudes, habits, skills, and specialized knowledge you'll have to have?

I can't answer that for you. Only you can answer it for yourself. And one way or another, you'll answer it for yourself—with either action or inaction.

Whether you're willing to pay the price of self-analysis and then work is up to you. But I must tell you . . . you're worth it, and the goals that you're capable of achieving are also worth it.

Spend a week on this chapter. Read it each day. Write down the new attitudes, habits, skills, and specialized knowledge you'll need in order to reach your goals. When all the required effort and discipline seem to be too much and the size of the job frustrates you (as it will), keep visualizing your goals.

The power of mentally enjoying your goals will carry you through the rough spots when the results don't seem worth the effort. Remember that all good things take time. Allow yourself time.

8

Managing Your Goal Progress

Achieving goals demands strong commitment, and I never think of strong commitment without thinking of an economics professor I had in college. He was a brilliant man, who several years earlier had reached the goal of earning a Ph.D. degree.

One day he explained to me that he'd grown up in extreme poverty. None of his family was educated. But his goal was to go to college and become a professor. He told me of saving up as much money as he could picking cotton. As it came time to enter college, his savings amounted to only about two hundred dollars. All his possessions fit into a paper sack.

He explained that his father had no money to give him but that a neighbor who operated a small fruit stand gave him a stalk of bananas to take with him. So off he went, hitchhiking, with a stalk of bananas and a paper sack. He told of his extreme embarrassment, hunger, and uncertainties. He told of the odd jobs he got in order to survive. No social life, no entertainment, no frills. But he stuck with it until he got a bachelor's degree, then a master's, and ultimately a Ph.D.

I'm sure that during the years it took him to do it, there were tens of thousands of high school graduates saying to themselves, "I'd love to go to college, but I can't afford it."

I have a good friend, Willard Tate, who is now a college professor. When I first knew him, he was a successful basketball coach in a junior college in Alabama. In fact, that year his team went to the national finals.

As I got acquainted with him, I was particularly impressed with his propensity for asking questions. He picked me apart with questions. "Who, what, where, why, when, how" came out of him like bullets. He had an extremely strong curiosity, which I interpreted as high-achievement drive and desire to learn.

From some of his other friends, I found out some interesting facts about Willard. He, too, came from a background of extreme poverty. When he came to college, he was married and had no money. To support himself and his family, he got a job picking up garbage in the early mornings, and then he would throw two paper routes. He'd get up around

4 A.M. each day, and then work after classes. How he survived defied any semblance of logic. But he did. In fact, he went on to get advanced degrees.

Our mutual friend also told me that when Willard began coaching the junior college basketball team they had no gym in which to practice. That didn't deter him, though. He got his team up at 5 A.M. and went to a rented high school gym to practice.

Difficulties didn't stop him. In fact, they probably strengthened him and made the journey more exciting and rewarding. You've known people like this—whose no-withdrawal commitment saw them through extreme difficulties.

MANY PEOPLE ARE UNWILLING TO GIVE TOTAL COMMITMENT

Since the early 1960s I've conducted hundreds of courses and seminars all over the world. I've talked intimately with thousands of people about their lives and goals. In almost every training session I've ever conducted, I've met at least one person who follows a classic pattern. At every break, they materialize nose-to-nose to me. They all ask the same kind of questions, like, "Have you read such and such a book?" Or "What do you think of so and so's theories?" Or "How do you explain your ideas compared with such and such a person?"

They love to discuss or argue ideas, concepts, or positions. But I only have to ask a couple of questions to discover that while they may know a lot of theory, they don't practice much of it.

I don't waste time with those people. As cynical as it sounds, I've found that there's little I can do to help them.

Content to dwell in the realms of philosophical discussions, they probably won't take action and perform the activities that are necessary to reach serious goals. That's sad, but true. Many people aren't willing to pay the price of high achievement.

Two or three years ago a young man came into my office who'd just gone into the life insurance business. I'd known him for a long time, he knew I carried a lot of life insurance, and I got the message that he thought I'd be a good prospect for a big sale.

Since I'd had the same thing happen a few million times before, I told him that one agent handled all of my life insurance. As I explained that, I also wished him the greatest success imaginable. I tried to say as nicely as I could that I probably wouldn't buy from someone who didn't have much experience anyway because I'd want to know my agent would be around to service my policies.

For about an hour I listened as he assured me that he was in the business to stay, that his company was the best there was, his manager was the best in the business, and that he'd set high goals—and would attain them.

I wished him luck and sincerely hoped he'd make it big because he was a nice young man. Six months later he was doing something else.

I once consulted with a sales organization that had 325 percent salesperson turnover per year. Many of their new recruits wouldn't last even a week. It was interesting, though, that when each one came out of a two-week training school they all set high sales-production goals. No one set goals to fail or bomb out.

Looking at the incredibly high dropout rate, I asked myself, "Why? Can't their products be sold?"

The answer was, "Sure they can be sold; many people sell them successfully."

"Then why don't all of these people who quit achieve the level of success they committed to in training?"

The answer is, of course, "They don't give total commitment."

HOW TO WASTE YOUR TIME READING THIS BOOK

If you've read this book to this point, you've either done the goal-setting and assessment activities I've suggested, or you've only read about them.

I've got to be honest and tell you that if you've only *read* the chapters, without taking *action* and performing the activities, you've wasted your time. You'll probably be no different than you were before reading this book.

Why am I so negative and critical? Well, first, because it's the truth and I don't want to gloss over that. And, second, because this chapter is meaningless unless it's acted upon.

Which finally gets me to the purpose of this chapter: The purpose of this chapter is to give you a simple strategy for managing your goal progress.

To do that, I'll suggest these four action guides to practice:

1. review goals,
2. proceed,
3. revise, or
4. recycle.

Let's think of each of these steps. You'll see how easy they are, and I hope you'll motivate yourself to take them.

STOP NOW AND ORGANIZE A GOAL BOOKLET

In Chapter 4 I suggested that you write down your goals in an active statement. If you haven't done this, I'd suggest you take the time *now*. Go back to Chapter 4, page 60, and respond to the questions I asked. Select your six most-important responses and put a target date on each. Then write each into an active statement as I instructed.

A simple way to record your goals is to take an 8½ × 11 sheet of paper and fold it three times—first, from top to bottom, forming a folded sheet that's 8½ inches wide and 5½ inches high. Then fold it from side to side, forming a folder that's 4¼ inches wide and 5½ inches high. Then fold it a third time from top to bottom forming a booklet that's 4¼ inches high by 2¾ inches wide.

If this sounds complicated, just get a piece of paper and try it. You'll see that it's really simple.

On your small 2¾ × 4¼ booklet you might want to put a label: MY GOALS. Then, on the first inside fold, you can write down your six goals.

On the second inside fold (the 5½ × 8½ fold), write the heading: STRATEGY FOR REACHING MY GOALS. Then, under that heading, write the numbers—spaced evenly on the left side of the page—1, 2, 3, 4, 5, 6. After each number, write down activities or subgoals that are necessary for reaching your six goals.

Then turn to the third inside fold to the 8½ × 11 sheet. It will have eight squares on it—four on the left side of the center and four on the right of center.

On the left four squares, write the heading BUILDING BE-

LIEF, and on the right four squares write STRENGTHS TO DEVELOP.

Under BUILDING BELIEF, label the four boxes: AFFIRMATIONS, VISUALIZATION, GRAPHIC REPRESENTATION, and ENVIRONMENTAL INFLUENCES.

Under the heading STRENGTHS TO DEVELOP, label the boxes ATTITUDES, HABITS, SKILLS, and SPECIALIZED KNOWLEDGE.

Now, don't get lazy on me. This sounds like a lot more work than it really is. Please stop reading and do these things *now! Do it now!*

Thank you, you'll be glad you did. Your time and trouble will pay off for you. This simple goal booklet, and other future ones you'll write in, can serve you well in the years ahead. They'll help you manage your goal progress.

REVIEW GOALS

The first action guide for managing your goal progress is to *review your goals.* You can do this by reading your goal booklet either daily or weekly.

Each time you read your booklet ask yourself some questions. Ask:

1. Where am I with this goal—what is my progress?
2. Are all my goals still important to me?
3. How can I best use my time?
4. What subgoals should I have already reached that will help take me to my main goals?

Next turn to the page heading, "Building Belief." Ask yourself these questions.

1. Am I doing my affirmations daily?
2. Am I daily visualizing my goals?
3. Do I have pictures, slogans, or symbols that remind me of my goal?
4. Do I choose people, places, things that will provide a supporting environment?

This is how you review your goals. Until this process is pretty well internalized into your habits, I'd recommend that you go through it daily. Then two or three times each week.

As you review your goals, you'll discover only three appropriate responses. For each of your goals, you'll want to:

1. proceed,
2. review, or
3. recycle.

PROCEED

You'll know when to *proceed* with your goal when you still want to achieve it, believe that it's possible, and are willing to keep building belief and developing the strengths to reach it.

In other words, your goal is still important to you. You still want to reach it but haven't had enough time. So you proceed. You keep building belief and developing the strengths you need—realizing that when everything comes together you'll either see your goal within reach or have reached it!

If you want to reach a goal, keep using this system. If your goal is truly realistic and doesn't conflict with your values or beliefs, you should one day reach it—even if now that seems impossible.

I'll never forget one evening in one of my classes about twenty years ago, when a young man set a goal to get a new Jaguar XKE twelve-cylinder sports convertible. He cut out a picture of one that had white paint and biscuit-colored leather upholstery. He'd just taken over a print shop that was all but broke. The shop was doing only four thousand to five thousand dollars monthly volume—almost nothing.

He set a goal for the car and promised himself that when the shop was doing volume of forty thousand dollars per month, and he had the cash to pay for the car, he'd get it. It seemed all but impossible to him. He was so far away from achieving the volume goal that it made the possibility of enjoying the Jaguar very remote.

One day, three or four years later, he came into my office, flipped a set of car keys on my desk, and said, "Come out and look at 'our' car!" He had a big grin on his face.

So we went out to the curb, and there, parked in a NO PARKING zone at the building entrance, was . . . you've got it! A brand-new, white with biscuit-colored leather, twelve-cylinder Jaguar XKE sports convertible. Just like the picture he'd cut out a few years earlier.

I drove it and felt the power and the smoothness of the gears and the smell of the English leather. But all that didn't equal his pride and excitement.

He explained to me what had happened in the years that had elapsed. How difficult the first ones had been. He had no money to buy inventory. Creditors hounded him. Some forced him to purchase on a cash with order basis. It was tough. But he hung in and persisted.

He told me how many evenings he'd close the shop and

sit down in his office exhausted from the pressures he had. He'd sit there and look at the picture of the Jaguar—telling himself that one day he'd have it. He'd fantasize about it. He'd visualize the power of it. How he would feel driving it on an open freeway. He'd mentally rub his hands over the supple leather. In his imagination he'd wax it and clean it. He went through these exercises almost daily.

At first, it seemed hopeless. He even felt guilty at times. "Why am I wasting time thinking about something I'll probably never have . . . or shouldn't have?" Or "Why am I wasting time daydreaming about an expensive car when I can't even pay my bills?"

All of these thoughts would run through his mind. But he persisted. And then one month, much later, his shop did forty thousand dollars in business. Then it began to average above that. Then he saved enough money to buy the car. It was a great example of persistence in goal achievement.

Incidentally, almost twenty years later, he still has the car, and it's worth more now than when he bought it. So it was not a bad investment. It all happened because he *proceeded.* He kept on working toward his goal because it remained important to him.

REVISE

The second appropriate response after you review your goals is to *revise* them. I'm always amazed how fast some goals come into reality after I set them. I often look back at goal booklets on which I've set goals in the past. Almost always most of them have happened—and often sooner than I expected.

Another discovery that usually strikes me is that many of

my goals had to be revised after initially setting them. They either had to be revised *up* or *down*. Often, I discover, after setting and working on goals for a while, that they aren't consistent with my values, my priorities, or some of my other goals. For these reasons, I need to revise them.

I set a goal several years ago to get a new Rolls-Royce. For several years, when I was doing seminars in Los Angeles or New York or Chicago, I'd go by the Rolls-Royce dealership and fantasize about owning one. But soon after setting the goal, I began to feel discomfort. I felt guilty and irresponsible. Then it dawned on me one day that it was causing some conflicts within me.

What kind of conflicts? Well, first, I live in a small West Texas city of a hundred fifty thousand people. Few of our friends even know what a Rolls-Royce is, much less want one. Then the thought of driving one down the streets created a much more ostentatious image than I wanted. I could hardly see myself driving up to church and teaching my Sunday School class.

Obviously, there was a problem, a conflict. The solution seemed to be one of these two options:

1. change my environment to one in which owning a car like that would be comfortable, or
2. change my goal to fit the environment in which I live.

So, I did the second one. I revised my goal by taking it off my list.

After you set your goals and have worked on them for a while, are there any that you need to change? If so, what do you need to change or revise about them?

Revising your goals may require raising or lowering them. Or it may call for you to drop them—to take them off your list altogether. Don't feel guilty for revising your goals. This shows progress. It's good.

It's normal for your goals to change as you change. As your values change, your goals will change. As your priorities change, your goals will change. As you reach goals, your new goals will change. All this is normal.

RECYCLE

The third appropriate response you can take after you review your goals is to *recycle*. When you recycle, you redefine your goals and go back through your Goal Achievement System. You do the following:

1. plan strategy,
2. build belief,
3. develop strengths, and
4. manage progress.

You may also recycle when you've had a lapse of interest or have once set a goal and later stalled out.

It's common to set a goal, be serious about it for a while, and then lose interest in it. Or maybe new events cause us to let it lapse from our priorities. Then sometime later we get excited about it again.

My wife and I have just purchased a townhouse in Scottsdale, Arizona, at a beautiful new development called the Phoenician. It's a dream come true for us. We first set a goal to do this well over ten years ago. We love the Phoenix area and have gone there each year for the last twenty years. We'd stay from four to five days to a month.

But with children growing up and then in college, financial ups and downs and other changes just kept causing the reality of it to escape us. Then about eighteen months ago, while spending a month there, we reset a goal to get a place there. We thought and talked about it for a year. Then a year later we made the decision to get it. It was a goal that had lapsed and years later we *recycled.*

It's common to lose interest in goals, or for experiences to force us to abandon them, only to later revive our interest in them. When this happens, we simply need to recycle and go through the Goal Achievement System again.

THE GOAL ACHIEVEMENT SYSTEM IS A SYSTEM

The Goal Achievement System that I've presented in these last five chapters forms a very powerful, workable system. When you follow the system as outlined and manage your progress, you'll discover that something will happen. In fact, you'll at times be amazed at how quickly some of your goals come into existence.

You'll find that this system is just that—a system! It will guide you into a step-by-step process. It has its own built-in checks and balances, its policing agents. It has its own internal guidance systems. It's fully functioning; all you have to do is punch the start-up button, activate, and maintain the system; and it'll work for you.

Now I've conducted enough seminars in goal setting to know some of the realities of getting people to follow this system. One common response I get is, "Yeah, well, this may all be true, but there's more to life than just reaching material goals!"

And I agree. I've used measurable, material examples throughout these chapters. But I've done it to be clear, specific, and tangible . . . and, I hope, to prove my point.

There's more to life than cars, houses, clothes, and money. I'll be the first to admit that. Spiritual dimensions and family and personal relationships are infinitely more important. But these inner qualities are also goals to attain, which you can use this system to attain.

We'll think about this in later chapters.

PRACTICE THIS SYSTEM UNTIL YOU DO THE STEPS AUTOMATICALLY

I'll quickly admit that this five-step system looks somewhat mechanical, with a lot of rules and guides. I've designed it that way for a purpose. The reason is so that nothing is left to chance. So that we cover all of the bases. So that any serious student will have all of the answers.

What I know from experience is that if you follow this system to the letter—defining specific goals and then working through the steps—you'll experience success. When you do, you'll *emotionally* believe in the process. You'll believe that it'll really work for you. Then, with time and experience, the whole Goal Achievement System will become more of an automatic process. You'll perform many of the steps unconsciously.

Achieving this mind-set will take time and practice, but with repetition you'll instinctively begin to think and act in a goal-focused way. I've shared this Goal Achievement System with many thousands of people. I've used it myself. I know it works. I know it'll work for you!

SUMMING UP

In this chapter I've shared with you ways with which you can manage your goal progress—how you can realize your goals.

I challenged you to make a commitment to your goals. I wrote that commitment means you'll do whatever is necessary to reach them. It's a no-withdrawal, persistent attitude.

Then I shared with you the following four action guides for managing your goal progress:

1. review goals,
2. proceed,
3. revise, or
4. recycle.

You learned to review your goal booklet daily, and that when you do, there'll be only three possible responses to take—proceed, revise, or recycle. You learned how to do these things.

I also shared with you the way you can take an 8½ × 11 sheet of paper and make a simple goal booklet. Remember, it sounds more complicated when you read about how to do it than it really is when you try it.

Please take time to make the booklet and follow my simple instructions about recording your goals, planning strategy, building belief, and developing strengths. When you do these activities, you'll receive almost immediate payoff.

Take a Saturday, or another day, off and work through the five steps. You'll find that it'll be a red-letter day in your climb toward greater success and self-fulfillment. You'll discover the rewards will be well worth the effort.

Part III

No man can learn what he has not preparation for learning.

—RALPH WALDO EMERSON

Part III

9

Releasing Your
Achievement Drive

Dr. David C. McClelland, professor of psychology at Harvard University, has spent many years studying what he calls Achievement Drive, or Need for Achievement. He has studied individuals, organizations, and societies. His basic conclusion is that achievement drive is one of the key factors in any successful accomplishment.

While Dr. McClelland coined the terms Achievement Drive, or Need for Achievement, we describe this quality by other terms, such as ambition, drive, desire to excel, will to win, or competitive nature.

In studying individuals, organizations, and nations, Dr. McClelland came to the conclusion that Achievement Drive is the multiplier of success. It doesn't just *add* to a person's skills or abilities, it *multiplies* them. And the higher it is, the greater it multiplies. He found that individuals, firms, or societies with high Achievement Drive find a way to excel and prosper regardless of their national resources or other factors or conditions.

Look at modern-day Japan as an example. They may soon own the world. While this is a bit of an exaggeration, it's phenomenal to see what this achieving society has done in the last twenty-five years. With few natural resources, they have become world leaders in finance, manufacturing, and trade.

Because of their achievement-oriented work ethic, their automobiles, once laughed at, now flood the world and rank highest in customer satisfaction and maintenance-free operation. They've set world-class standards in electronics equipment and cameras. They now own many of the biggest banks in the world. They enjoy an unbelievable cash flow.

Contrast them with other nations, especially ones with similar natural resources, and the main factor that sets them apart is their attitude of achievement.

Look at organizations today that succeed, and you'll see a certain corporate culture of high achievement. IBM, Hewlett-Packard, Nordstrom, as well as other companies large and small, have enjoyed outstanding success as a result of a carefully built culture of high achievement. Their leaders are people with high Achievement Drive. High achievers—

individuals, companies, or nations—find ways to succeed even in tough markets or conditions.

Since I train salespeople to be more productive, I've searched for many years for the reason why some people do well and others don't. Why does one person sell ten times as much as another person, who apparently has similar skills, aptitudes, and intelligence? Why does a person who doesn't seem to be too gifted succeed?

Recently, a young man came to me wanting to market our sales and customer-service training programs. In questioning him, I didn't detect what I thought was sufficient experience, so I discouraged him. When I didn't give him as much positive encouragement as he wanted, he pulled closer to me, looked me squarely in my eye, and said, "But you don't understand! I will be successful marketing your programs. I'll do whatever I have to do to succeed! I'll be one of your best people!"

This young man said this quietly, not arrogantly or boastfully. Somehow I knew he meant it. I could feel his strong achievement drive. He'll make it in our business.

I'll never forget a story a friend told me many years ago. He was a manager for a life insurance agency, and one day a character who looked like a cowboy walks into his office and asks for a job selling life insurance. The fellow was dressed in Levi's, boots, a Western shirt, and a ten-gallon hat.

"What experience have you had selling?" my friend asked him.

"None" was the reply.

"What kind of work have you done?" was the next question.

"I worked on a ranch for several years . . . and out at the cattle auction."

"At the cattle auction? What did you do there, work in the business office?"

"No, I worked the cattle."

"Oh, I see," my friend said, kindly, searching for a nice way to brush the man off. "And what makes you think you can sell life insurance?"

The cowboy looked at him very seriously and said, "Because I work hard and people trust me."

Again the manager tried to get rid of the man, but the cowboy wouldn't allow that to happen. "You'd have to pass an insurance exam," he told him.

"I figured I would."

Well, to make a long story short, the cowboy passed the exam and began to produce sales on a very consistent basis. He didn't sell big policies, but he sold lots of smaller ones.

Amazed at the success of the man, my friend asked him one day: "How come all your policies are ten-thousand-dollar policies, and how do you sell so many?"

Very seriously, the cowboy explained his success. He said, "I just go out to the ranch and to the cattle auction and talk to my old friends. First, I ask 'em how much life insurance they have. Whatever they say, I say, 'That's not enough.' Then they always ask me how much is enough, and I tell them they need ten thousand more.

"They always ask how much it will cost, and so I tell 'em. As soon as I do that, I tell 'em to sign this application where I've drawn an *X*. I call on a lot of people, and since they all trust me, they all sign. That's how I sell as much as I do!"

As it turned out, the cowboy had an unbelievably strong

Achievement Drive. He probably explained his success well when he said, "I work hard and people trust me!"

He proves what Dr. McClelland wrote, that people, firms, or nations lacking resources but with high Achievement Drive, manage to find a way to succeed.

ACHIEVEMENT DRIVE IS RELEASED FROM WITHIN

This is a most significant point. Achievement Drive is released from within, not poured in from without. You don't get or acquire Achievement Drive; you release it. My point is that the capacity for it *already* exists within you, waiting to get out. Almost every example that I've shared in this book proves this point.

The problem for most people is that this dimension lies frozen within them. It never gets out, never gets released. Most people live out the roles handed them by their early environment. They usually fill their expected roles the rest of their lives—unless someone or something intervenes and changes their course.

Since the early 1960s I've conducted training courses that were primarily aimed at helping people discover their talents and abilities. The basic tools we use are goal setting and activity commitment; heavily sprinkled with positive reinforcement, total acceptance of each individual, lots of praise and encouragement.

We help people shatter their small, self-imposed paradigms—their mental boundaries—and select new, enlarged ones. We see people change emotionally. When this happens, their whole lives change.

In training courses we've found that it takes a person three to four weeks of practicing action guides to break their old habits or routines. A disruption has to happen before significant paradigm shifts can be made. Unless a disruption occurs, people aren't moved out of their ruts of comfortable behavior.

We've found that by getting people to set desirable goals and encouraging them to reach them, their self-beliefs gradually change. We give lots of positive reinforcement and help them discover levels of strength and creativity that are silently waiting to come out of them.

How to Release Achievement Drive

After exposure to tens of thousands of people whom I've personally trained, and second-hand exposure to hundreds of thousands of people who my trainers have trained, I have one extremely strong belief. I'm 100 percent sure it's correct. It is that any normal person has many levels of capability for achievement. That actual achievement depends on a person's *desire, drive,* or *need* for it.

My belief is that this capacity is infinite. It's infinite because it's part of the Creative Power given us by our Creator. The key to claiming this power is our own *belief.* It's as simple as that. It's also as profound and complex as that.

Reflect on this statement and you'll discover this is a thought that I've repeated many times in this book. I've done so purposely—to present this concept in as many ways as I could, hoping the repetition would help you internalize it as an emotional understanding.

But let's get practical. I don't understand complex concepts unless they're spelled out in black and white for me. So let's do that. Here are some specific ways to release achievement from within yourself:

1. Get excited about the *possibility* of enjoying greater achievement.
2. Set goals that are beyond your current level of achievement.
3. Daydream about your goals.
4. Reward yourself frequently.
5. Listen to and read self-help cassettes and books.
6. Associate with people who also are high achievers.

Get Excited about the Possibility of Enjoying Greater Achievement

It all begins with hope—thinking in terms of possibilities, entertaining thoughts like "What if?" "Why not?" and "If others can, I can also!"

I'll never forget how exciting it was when this began to happen to me in the early 1960s. I owned a retail furniture store. It was going nowhere. Don Williams, my insurance agent, gave me a well-worn record called *The Strangest Secret* by Earl Nightingale.

Earl talked about goals and possibilities. The emotional tone he projected in the recording had a deep influence on me. He talked about believing. He quoted the Scriptures in which Christ said to his disciples, "If Thou canst believe, all things are possible for him who believes."

I listened to that recording each morning before opening my store. I began to see beyond the four walls of that store into the vast world beyond. Suddenly two or three people came into my life who were also seekers and learners.

I'll never forget those months of intense excitement when *hope for a greater tomorrow* began to grow in me. There were strong counteremotions of uncertainty and anxiety about the future, but this conflict only served to make the growth process more exhilarating.

One of my goals in writing this book is to get you excited about your possibilities of enjoying greater achievement.

SET GOALS THAT ARE BEYOND YOUR CURRENT LEVEL OF ACHIEVEMENT

I've said it before, but not in this exact context, that your Achievement Drive is expanded by setting goals that are beyond your current level of achievement.

Now let me stop and deal with a very important question you probably have about goal setting. The question is, "Should I set big goals or small ones?" Some experts say, "Aim high!" Others advise, "Be very realistic." What's the difference and what's right?

What's right? Well, *both!* We need to set high goals to challenge us and stretch our minds; while at the same time setting short-range goals that are just beyond where we are now.

Longer-range, aim-high goals help create visions of the big picture. They widen our horizons and expand our outlook. They're very important. But long-term goals can also be a cop-out, unless they're supported by short-range, here-and-now goals.

Short-range goals are important because they offer frequent gratification. Most of us won't work long unless there's some kind of gratification. We want some sort of payoff. Similarly, there needs to be the promise of frequent rewards in order for us to release our inner Achievement Drive.

Since success breeds success, the success of achieving short-term goals gives us the thrill of victory and adds fuel to our Achievement Drive.

DAYDREAM ABOUT YOUR GOALS

In one of the most often-quoted statements from Dr. Maxwell Maltz's *Psycho-Cybernetics,* he wrote, "Our subconscious minds can't tell the difference between a real experience and one that has been vividly imagined." He then goes on to talk about visualizing success.

In our Goal Achievement System you learned to visualize your success by mentally picturing yourself already in possession of your goals. This is creative daydreaming. Many high achievers use this technique.

A few years ago, I was in Chicago in the office of wealthy insurance man W. Clement Stone. We drove for dinner from his office to his home, a huge Mediterranean mansion on Sheridan Drive, with the back facing Lake Michigan. As we were walking up to his front door, I asked him, "When did you first really believe that you'd live in a home like this?"

I suppose I was expecting more of a thought-out, complex answer than the one I got. He quickly responded, "Since I was a child reading Horatio Alger books."

That was it! Point quickly made. No hesitation. For some reason this hit me like a thunderbolt, that he really did think as a young man that he'd live in a place like that. But there's more to the story.

Those close to Mr. Stone, now nearing ninety—and as alert and active as anyone half his age—know of another interesting habit of his. It's what he calls his "daily planning and thinking time."

In this daily period of about thirty minutes, he relaxes and mentally reviews his goals. He visualizes reaching them. He thinks about the strategy of reaching them. He reaches a relaxed state where he mentally reviews his goals but also receives renewal of energy from the experience. He arises tremendously refreshed from the experience.

I know another man whose net worth is close to the $100-million mark who has this daily habit. He spends fifteen to twenty minutes in a warm shower each morning mentally picturing his goals. His creative mind flows fully—planning his strategy, anticipating problems and solutions—visualizing the joys of reaching his goals. This habit releases more and more Achievement Drive from him and fuels him for very productive days.

Many people who have been thought to be gifted, creative geniuses, aren't really natural geniuses at all. They have simply learned to tap into the power of this creative energy channel of visualization.

From writings about Thomas Edison, we can discern this practice. He'd work in his shop around the clock—stopping occasionally for catnaps. At other times, when stymied with a problem, he'd drift off into a relaxed half-conscious state after thinking intensely about the problem. He found that this often yielded solutions. Answers would pop into his mind, seemingly out of nowhere. It was interesting how Edison used this Creative Power within him to solve problems and reach goals.

A reporter was once interviewing him and referred to him as a genius. Edison corrected him by responding, "Genius? Me? Hardly!" He went on to explain the reason for his apparent genius was that he'd learned to use his Creative Powers—powers that everyone has.

The article was entitled, "You Too, Can Be a Genius!" The thrust was that anyone who discovers and uses the creative abilities that we all have, and who will polish them with years of use, can achieve things that appear to be way out of the range of normal, nongeniuses.

REWARD YOURSELF FREQUENTLY

Another way to release your Achievement Drive is to reward yourself frequently. Give yourself specific rewards for achieving small goals. I've found this to be very helpful in motivating myself to achieve goals and to add excitement to the process.

A new briefcase, a gold pen, a new article of clothing, something for your home, a trip, time off, an evening of relaxation, a special dinner—these are only a few of the ways by which you reward yourself for achieving short-term goals.

As you look for rewards, try to think of things that you'd like to have, things you wouldn't go out and buy. Luxury items that you wouldn't ordinarily buy make great self-incentives.

Personally, I don't like to spend money. But I like nice things. So there are a lot of things I'd like to have that I won't buy for myself. These become great rewards for reaching goals or making sales.

When you reach a goal, you might also want to consider buying your spouse something he or she wants, which isn't within your normal range of expenditures. When I signed the contract on my previous book, I went into a shop on Fifth Avenue in New York and bought my wife a ring. It rewarded her for the times I neglected her while writing the book.

What rewards can you give yourself for reaching goals? As you answer this question, and then go through rewarding yourself, you'll unconsciously *condition* yourself to have higher Achievement Drive. Do this frequently and you'll benefit with the enjoyment of larger and larger goals.

LISTEN TO AND READ SELF-HELP CASSETTES AND BOOKS

I remember clearly when I bought a copy of *Success Through a Positive Mental Attitude* by Napoleon Hill and W. Clement Stone. I read it several times. It kept making this statement: "Whatever the mind of man can conceive and believe, it can achieve!"

At first, I intellectually believed it but didn't emotionally understand it. I'm still discovering new levels of meaning in the statement. But the book changed my life. It gave me direction and hope and helped me develop a more positive mind-set.

Since then, I've read hundreds of self-help books and constantly listen to positive, self-building audiocassettes. I've discovered that I need the constant support of positive messages. There's enough in the world that's negative and oppressive. Instead of gloom, doom, and destruction, we all need to be exposed to messages of hope, optimism, and positive expectations.

I recently had lunch with a university president who had weathered some severe storms of reorganization. Staff and faculty adjustments had been made that caused many rocks to be thrown at him. He even received several death threats.

But through all the problems emerged a vital university that's offering an excellent education to its students.

I asked him how he stayed so positive and up. He told me that he regularly spends at least thirty minutes each day reading self-help books or listening to motivational audiocassettes. He explained that his daily feeding on these positive messages kept him going and believing in the quality of university he wanted to build.

I like to challenge people to budget from 2 percent to 5 percent of their incomes on their own continuing education, to spend it on books, tapes, seminars, and other educational opportunities. My belief is that if anyone will do this, and *apply* the knowledge they gain, that their income and success will increase in a multiplied way. I know people who have done this and have said that it works. Since I began doing this, my income has increased at least fifty times what it was when I started.

Are you willing to try this exciting experiment? Are you willing to gamble and prove to yourself whether it'll work for you or not? You can find an ample selection of self-help books at almost any bookstore. Many have cassette tapes, too.

You'll find that these ideas of exposing your mind to self-help action books and cassettes will cause increased amounts of Achievement Drive to be released from within you. Many people have been motivated to higher achievement by reading and then applying success principles found in self-help books.

ASSOCIATE WITH PEOPLE WHO ARE ALSO HIGH ACHIEVERS

Dr. M. Norvel Young and Dr. William S. Banowsky, both high achievers, sparked each other's Achievement Drive so much that together they believed they could build a new world-class university. This was in the 1970s when schools of higher learning were folding up all over the country.

The chancellor and president respectively of Pepperdine University in Los Angeles, they found themselves hemmed in by decaying neighborhoods close to the Watts district in that city.

With little more than a vision, enthusiasm, and lots of friends, they built a new university on the beautiful hills of Malibu, which initially was to cost around $75 million and later to cost much more.

To stand on the side of the mountain in Malibu and scan this incredibly beautiful new school, with the Pacific Ocean in the background, is awesome. The fact that two men with a belief could achieve that always staggers me when I see it.

One of the secrets of releasing high Achievement Drive is to associate with people who have high Achievement Drive. I've observed as a general principle that if I take the people I closely associate with, average their incomes, they'll closely match what mine is. Think about that for a moment.

What it suggests is that if you want to earn a certain income figure, or reach other goals, associate with people whose average achievements are about what you'd like yours to be. Now, don't think too one-dimensionally about this—don't think I'm just talking about money. I'm talking about anything—money, knowledge, spiritual understanding, special interests—whatever your goal areas are.

Here's a principle worth remembering: When we associate with people who are achieving what we'd like to achieve, it helps us build belief that we can perform on that level.

I mentioned earlier that I'm a member of the National Speakers Association. We get together two to three times a year for workshops and conventions. It's a group of very high achievers. We visit and share ideas. We also have ongoing relationships. It's a mind-expanding experience.

On a local level, I associate with high achievers. My closest friends locally are a doctor, a lawyer, and an entrepreneur. I schedule lunches with other local high achievers.

How can you associate with people who are performing on the level that you'd like to perform? Here are some suggestions:

1. Schedule lunches with high achievers—tell them you want to learn from them. Often successful people will gladly teach others who sincerely want to learn.
2. Join civic groups in which business leaders gather.
3. Form study groups and jointly read self-help books, then share ideas.

Now I can't leave this subject without being a bit negative in order to nail my point down. It's this: *Don't associate with losers!*

Here's a helpful hint. In the next thirty days every time you're with a group of people that you've chosen to be with, ask yourself, "Are these people performing on a level that I want to perform on, or is it lower?" Ask yourself that question for thirty days and you'll be amazed at the awareness it'll cause you to develop.

WHAT IS YOUR CURRENT LEVEL OF ACHIEVEMENT DRIVE?

We can hardly talk about the value of achievement in multiplying your success, as well as ways to increase it, without taking a good look in the mirror and assessing what it is now.

The following questions ask you to rate yourself in several areas. This isn't designed to be a validated, objective instrument, but only to give you a quick look at yourself . . . and mainly to make you think.

Please read each question and score it from 0 to 10. Answer each question quickly, without giving any study to it.

ACHIEVEMENT DRIVE PROFILE

The following questions ask about your life-style and work preferences. Please circle the appropriate measurement to each question from 0 to 10: 0 indicating that the statement is *never* descriptive of you; 10 indicating that the statement is *always* descriptive. Or choose a number in between that's most descriptive of you.

Now, you can easily skew this to get any answer you want, so be honest with yourself. Again, these qustions are designed to make you think rather than being an accurate assessment of your drive.

1. I value job opportunity much more than job security.
   NEVER 0 1 2 3 4 5 6 7 8 9 10 ALWAYS

2. Most of my family members are high achievers.
   NEVER 0 1 2 3 4 5 6 7 8 9 10 ALWAYS

3. Most of my friends are high achievers.
   NEVER 0 1 2 3 4 5 6 7 8 9 10 ALWAYS

4. I have written goals in two or more areas of my life.
   NEVER 0 1 2 3 4 5 6 7 8 9 10 ALWAYS

5. I work around several high achievers.
   NEVER 0 1 2 3 4 5 6 7 8 9 10 ALWAYS

6. I regularly read or listen to self-help materials.
   NEVER 0 1 2 3 4 5 6 7 8 9 10 ALWAYS

7. In my spare time I do work-related activities.
   NEVER 0 1 2 3 4 5 6 7 8 9 10 ALWAYS

8. I set moderately difficult goals.
   NEVER 0 1 2 3 4 5 6 7 8 9 10 ALWAYS

9. I've already achieved goals I set during the last year.
   NEVER 0 1 2 3 4 5 6 7 8 9 10 ALWAYS

10. I set my own goals.
    NEVER 0 1 2 3 4 5 6 7 8 9 10 ALWAYS

11. I think my job gives me unlimited opportunities.
    NEVER 0 1 2 3 4 5 6 7 8 9 10 ALWAYS

12. I focus on the value I can create for others.
    NEVER 0 1 2 3 4 5 6 7 8 9 10 ALWAYS

13. I have a daily habit of fantasizing about reaching goals, making sales, or enjoying rewards.
    NEVER 0 1 2 3 4 5 6 7 8 9 10 ALWAYS

14. I have an open-ended, no-limitations opportunity.
    NEVER 0 1 2 3 4 5 6 7 8 9 10 ALWAYS

15. I'm often rewarded for short-term successes.
    NEVER 0 1 2 3 4 5 6 7 8 9 10 ALWAYS

16. I spend time each week with friends talking about goals and personal growth.
    NEVER 0 1 2 3 4 5 6 7 8 9 10 ALWAYS

17. I enjoy solving problems.
    NEVER 0 1 2 3 4 5 6 7 8 9 10 ALWAYS

18. I'm always looking for new ways to get things done.
    NEVER 0 1 2 3 4 5 6 7 8 9 10 ALWAYS

Now that you've scored these questions, fill in numbers in the following blanks.

Total of all 18 items _____
Divided by 18 = _____

If your responses are somewhat accurate, here are some descriptions of your level.

Low   0–2
Fair   3–4
Average   5–6
High   7–8
Extremely High   9–10

Again, this is only designed to make you think and to assess yourself.

SUMMING UP

The purpose of this chapter has been to make these major points:

1. Our Achievement Drive determines and *multiplies* our success and goal achievement.
2. Achievement Drive is released from within; it isn't poured in from without.
3. Achievement Drive can be released when we
   a. get excited about the possibility of enjoying goal achievement;
   b. set goals that are just beyond our current level of achievement;
   c. daydream about our goals;
   d. reward ourselves frequently;
   e. listen to and read self-help cassettes and books; and
   f. associate with people who are also high achievers.

Understanding and taking action on the concepts presented in this chapter can cause your own Achievement Drive to move upward.

Of course, it all begins with your desire, and then the commitment to practice these ideas.

10

Deciding What
You Stand For

A couple of years ago, Bill Brooks, an associate, and I were
conducting a sales training program for executives from several different firms. One of the executives came up to us and
suggested that he'd be willing to influence his firm to buy
our program . . . if we'd give him a "finder's fee." He had
dressed up a phrase that I'd always heard called a "kick-
back."

Without hesitating, Bill shot back, "No. We don't do

business that way." The man was obviously surprised at that response and reacted in a condescending manner at our business naïveté. The look he gave us was, "Who are these hicks?"

As was expected, he gave our seminar and program a poor rating. A few months later he was terminated from his job and had a difficult time finding another. Meanwhile, Bill and I made a lot of money—honestly.

It's my strong belief that ultimately our success is determined by what we stand for—our values, priorities, ethics—our character. Knowledge, skill, and circumstances do not control your long-term success as much as who you are, what you stand for, *what* guides you live by. Yes, I know there are people who are amoral, cold, and self-serving, who seem to be doing well. But study their lives and you'll usually see excesses or blind spots that in time short-circuit their real happiness.

I can't rise above who I am. My achievements will ultimately be consistent with what I stand for. In the scheme of things, the goals I reach and maintain will be related to the ethical standards I set for myself. Nature ultimately balances all of our scales, allowing no long-term inequities. I can't be one thing and live something else any more than I can be and not be.

All around us we see proof of these natural laws. Just in the months I've been writing this book, I've seen Wall Street traders convicted of insider trading, presidential advisers convicted of influence peddling, presidential candidates caught in compromising situations, and evangelists' corruption exposed to the world.

But essentially the same things happen all the time. It may be the actor or actress who can't handle the rush of fame, or the athlete who can't handle the big money, or the local politician who can't handle easy opportunities. Many people's lives fall apart because of their lack of balance . . . or congruence . . . or integrity.

For these reasons, it's my belief that we need to balance the goals we set against the standards by which we choose to live our lives.

WE'RE ALL MULTIDIMENSIONAL BEINGS

So far in this book I've kept the subject on achieving goals. I've used examples that were measurable, tangible ones. I realize that in reading it, you might get the idea that I'm advocating a single-dimensional, materialistic existence. You may think that I think that the chief values in life are material things—cars, money, homes, etc.

Nothing could be further from the truth! The material nature is only one dimension, and we're multidimensional people. Our dimensions are

1. physical,
2. mental,
3. emotional, and
4. spiritual

I'm *physical*—I exist, I eat, I sleep, I work, I drive cars, I make monthly payments, I wear clothes, I live in a house.

I'm *mental*—I think, I remember lists, I do math, I spell words, I read books.

I'm *emotional*—I feel, I laugh, I cry, I hurt, I enjoy, I care, I worry, I hope.

I'm *spiritual*—I am, I love, I forgive, I accept forgiveness, I pray, I seek a Higher Power, I create, I heal.

VALUES—WHAT'S TEMPORARY
AND WHAT'S PERMANENT?

When I sat down and began to contemplate the vast question "What do I stand for?" I became awed at its significance. As I begin to answer the question, I immediately have to distinguish between what's *temporary* and what's *permanent.* Then, consciously or unconsciously, I have to answer for myself, "What's more important to me—temporary things or permanent things?"

The reality is that I live out my life answering this question, whether I realize it or not. I remember many experiences that prove this.

During my senior year in high school, when most of us were thinking about going to college, it was a difficult decision for many of us. For me, it boiled down to this: Did I get a job in the oil fields making what at the time seemed to be a lot of money, or did I want to go to college and barely scrape by for four years?

I remember one of the guys dropping out before he finished his senior year, getting a job and buying a brand-new 1950 yellow Mercury convertible. I'm sure that it took about all of his money to make the car payments, but, boy, was he the big wheel around school. He whizzed by after classes were out, giving us all sufficient reason to be jealous of him. It was a real temptation to opt for instant gratification. And many of the kids did.

Three or four years later, I saw the guy who'd bought the yellow convertible. Guess what? He still had it. And it wasn't bright and shiny anymore! Nor were girls hanging off it anymore! It struck me then that he'd made a bad decision.

It was a lesson that had a big impact on me—even at that age. It made me assess the value of a college education. I see now that the value of the lesson wasn't so much what I had learned, but the expansion of my own mental paradigm. My goals, ambitions, and expectations were greatly enlarged.

I didn't identify it that way at the time, but the value of one choice was temporary. It eventually got dents and wore out. The other was more permanent. It's served me in many ways since then.

Since then I've made many choices. Choices like:

1. Whom shall I marry?
2. Where shall I live?
3. Whom do I want for friends?
4. What will I do with my time?
5. What will I do with my money?
6. What values will I attempt to instill in my children?
7. What do I want my life to count for?
8. What do I believe about a Divine Creator?
9. What basic standard will I not compromise?
10. What do I put my trust in?

As I reflect, most of the choices I make involve choosing something *temporary* or something *permanent.* The argument isn't which is *right,* but which is more *enduring.*

TV evangelists soundly condemn materialism, while at the same time begging for money. But it seems to me that Christ didn't condemn materialism, rather he simply cast it aside as temporary—not of permanent value. To him it was a case of priorities. He said, "Render unto Caesar that which belongs to him, and render to God that which belongs to him." Christ taught values, attitudes, and priorities.

So without belaboring the point, let me again say that our values begin to be set by choosing between what's temporary and what's permanent.

When we look at it in those simple terms, we see that we often opt for temporary things. We do because it usually offers the quickest gratification.

WE OPT FOR INSTANT GRATIFICATION

Think about it for a moment. We do opt for temporary things because they provide us with quicker gratification. We opt for the physical rather than spiritual because it has more immediate payoff. We opt to enjoy now and pay later for the same reason.

Give a teenager a choice between a college education or seventy-five thousand dollars cash *now* and we'd have a lot of takers for the money. Give professional football players the choice between something that will take away the pain now, and make life wonderfully euphoric, and some of them will accept it—choosing instant gratification.

Recently I heard an interview with a well-known ex-professional football great whose life had been blighted by cocaine. When asked why he took it, he replied, "Because it was there." Then, when asked how it felt at first, he said, "Wonderful! Like free falling through space!" But then the crash came, he hit the ground and splattered. Some incredible talents were wasted.

I've had several interviews with Tom Landry, coach of the Dallas Cowboys. Though he certainly has not been without his ups and downs, I've been very impressed with his sense of values. The first time I visited with him, I sold him some cassette tapes on personal development. We talked about the power of goal setting and how, through it, players could achieve greater heights of play.

One of his questions was, "If you're saying that each person has unlimited potential, how does this fit with the Spirit of God that dwells within us?"

I wish I could say that I had a quick, profound answer. I didn't, but his question sure made me think. Then what he talked about the next few minutes told me a great deal about his values and priorities—which were extremely impressive.

A few years later, I saw a television interview with him just after losing the Super Bowl. The reporter asked him a question that assumed Landry would be devastated by the loss. Landry's response also showed his high sense of priorities. He replied, "We hate to lose. But winning the Super Bowl isn't the most important thing in the world to me." He went on to explain that his spiritual commitment was the most important thing in the world to him.

PRIORITIES

My priorities are what's most important to me . . . the order in which I value things.

Many people don't consciously identify their priorities, but their actions do. We all reveal our priorities by our actions. It's cause and effect—priorities, actions. I have a good friend, Dave Warren, who is a person I greatly admire and appreciate. For thirty-five years he was the president of a bank. He was the essence of success: highly respected, high integrity, model person, and wealthy!

A couple of years ago he was on a roll financially. He had about a million and a half in his home, an apartment in

Dallas, a ski lodge in northern New Mexico, a home in the Biltmore Estates in Phoenix. He had a Rolls-Royce, a couple of classic Mercedes-Benzs, a Jaguar, a BMW, and a King Air plane that took him about anywhere he wanted to go for trips and weekends. His net worth was over $20 million.

In the midst of all of this wealth, he was still a nice, spiritually discerning person. I greatly admired his values. He was a real giver, helping anyone who needed help. Then the oil crash came. His bank went under. He lost most everything he had, ending up with a negative net worth of several million dollars.

I saw him and called him frequently. I was amazed at how well he handled the problems he had. Many people have jumped off the top of twenty-story buildings after losing much less than he did.

I asked him why he looked so good and how he handled so well all of the banging he took. His response was that it had been very difficult and humiliating, but the money he had wasn't the most important thing in his life anyway—the Lord is!

His life is testimony to the priorities he's chosen. He understands *temporary* and *permanent*. His actions prove it.

Inadvertently, we all choose what's most important to us. Our actions then reveal our choice.

Many years ago, my father owned a small furniture and appliance store in an older, low-income part of the city. I was there one day when a retired woman who lived around the corner came into the store, screaming, "I'm calling the sheriff . . . my renter owes me seven dollars and I want the sheriff to come out and collect it."

She was furious. Screaming bad words and insults, she

had completely lost any sense of rationality. Not only had she ruined her own day, but she didn't contribute a great deal to the people in the store either.

I remember thinking that she had sold herself, emotionally, for seven dollars. I've thought of that experience many times when it would have been easy to get angry about someone owing me money. As I've thought of that experience, I've asked myself, "Her price for losing emotional control was seven dollars . . . what's mine?"

My priorities are expressed many ways—decisions I make, directions I choose, emotions I select.

It was in 1972 that I learned another good lesson about selecting emotional priorities. I was standing at the front entrance of the New York Hilton waiting for Dr. and Mrs. Maxwell Maltz to walk down and pick me up for dinner.

Standing beside me was a couple about the same age as the Maltzes. They were hurling abuses and verbal insults at each other so strongly that I shuddered. Their words dripped with poison—hateful and demeaning. I could hardly handle it emotionally.

I stepped outside the door to get away from them and looked across the street and saw the doctor and Anne crossing it. Arm in arm, they looked like newlyweds. The contrast had a profound effect on me. I remember thinking that both couples had made a choice. A priority had just been demonstrated.

The last time I had dinner with the Maltzes, before he died so suddenly, was at the restaurant in the Park Lane Hotel. We were laughing and the doctor broke into song, "Give my regards to Broadway . . . remember me to . . ."

Then he told me this story. He said that a couple of weeks

before, they had eaten there and then went back to their apartment only to find the elevators not working.

"What did you do?" I asked.

"We came back here and checked into a room and spent the night." Anne answered.

"In the raw!" the doctor chimed in.

"It was sooo romantic," she cooed.

The doctor looked at me, grinned, and then cut his eyes northeasterly. He looked like a kid who had just gotten his first kiss and didn't care if the whole world knew about it.

Priorities. Choices. Decisions. We all make them.

CHARACTER

Ralph Waldo Emerson eloquently expressed my own thoughts on character in these words from his essay on spiritual laws. "Human character evermore publishes itself. The most fugitive deed and word, the mere air of doing a thing, the intimated purpose, expresses character. If you act you show character: if you sit still, if you sleep, you show it."

We commonly use the word *character* to indicate that there are levels of behavior below which I will not go. The word encompasses several other virtues—integrity, dependability, discipline, honesty, sincerity, truthfulness.

In working with athletes and coaches, I've heard the word *character* used many times. I've seen kids who didn't seem to have the talent, but who had character, do well. I've seen others who had all kinds of natural ability—but who wouldn't show up for classes, would be late for practice, would not study—not make it. They lacked character.

It may well be that in modern times this seemingly old-fashioned virtue is scorned as unsophisticated and outdated.

But that's wrong. I've seen people who had incredible skills, abilities, and potential rise and fall. Their fall was almost always due to some character flaw. They couldn't handle their appetites. They couldn't handle their egos. They couldn't handle the ease of which things seemed to come to them because of their magnetic personalities. They opted for instant gratification. They chose the temporary rather than the permanent.

I had an associate once who was one of the most gifted speakers I'd ever heard. In two minutes he could capture an audience. He was wonderful at telling stories. He could make you laugh; he could make you cry. People never tired of hearing his stories. Many times he told me that his goal was to be the best speaker in the world, which of course would be pretty difficult to prove. It's ironic, but he could have been one of the best. He could . . . if he'd had more integrity.

It was so easy for him to convince people, that he fell into the trap of telling people what he thought they wanted to hear. He saw no need to consistently tell the truth. He also had a problem with women. He couldn't leave them alone. The ease of this, as well as the ego gratification that resulted, got him into a lot of trouble. He also saw no real need to pay some of his bills.

It wasn't long before he moved on, due to several problems he'd created. He'd been moving on most of his life and will probably be moving on the rest of it. It was a sad waste of talent.

In my professional career, I've seen many gifted people take the easy route. Their natural gifts made it easy for them to wing it and get by. Whether it was the gift of persuading people or an athletic gift, it allowed them to take the easy road and compromise effort or integrity.

I've seen highly talented people peak out and not go any further. Strange as it sounds, it's often the people who don't have a lot of natural ability, but who work and discipline themselves, who make it big. They do because the work and discipline causes them to build character.

In the Scriptures, the apostle Paul speaks to this issue of character. In the fifth chapter of Romans, he gives us some insight into how it's developed. He writes: "Not only so, but we also rejoice in our sufferings, because we know that suffering produces perseverance; perseverance, character; and character, hope." Perseverance produces character. This explains why some people don't have it.

Look around you at people you know who have high integrity. I'll bet that you'll also discover that much of their moral fiber, or character, has been strengthened in the blast furnace of adversity, that they've persevered through trials and difficulties. Because of discipline, commitment, and steadfastness, they've developed their strength. And it explains why they're where they are.

One of my best friends and business partner, Bernard Petty, is the essence of character and integrity. Everyone who knows him knows that when he says something, you can take it to the bank and deposit it. We've been doing deals for almost twenty years and have *zero* problems, disagreements, or conflicts—with nothing but a handshake.

An outstanding high school athlete in the late 1940s, he was recruited by many universities. He chose Texas A & M and went there on a football scholarship. He started and played both ways his freshman year. But then tragedy struck his life. He found out that he had a nerve degeneration problem in his eyes. The doctors sadly advised him to quit school, and added that he'd probably go blind in time.

Crushed and destroyed, he left school and exiled himself on his family's ranch for several years—trying to put his shattered life together. Then he met LaVerne, one of the most positive people in the world. They got married, and she was all he needed to turn his many strengths into a productive direction.

He got into the wholesale gasoline business and did well. He has excellent business savvy. There's no doubt in my mind that much of his outstanding character has been forged by his physical problem. He hasn't gone blind. Although he has poor vision, he can drive in his hometown and carry on his business functions.

I've lived almost fifty-five years now and I've noticed this one fact: As people show consistency and steadiness through adversity, a beauty and depth appear in them that other people don't have.

ETHICS

Another inner decision that we all make as we travel through life is, "What ethics will I abide by as I conduct my life."

Our ethics are standards of conduct—guidelines we go by —values we won't violate. Ethics is a big word in business today. I sat next to a man on a plane recently whose firm conducted ethics seminars for huge companies. He told me that the Department of Defense had mandated that military contractors all undergo ethics training. *What an interesting paradox,* I thought to myself.

Archie B. Carroll, professor of management at the University of Georgia, writing an article entitled "In Search of the Moral Manager" in the March/April 1987 issue of *Business Horizons,* writes:

Ethics and morality are back on the front page as a result of the Ivan Boesky, General Dynamics, General Electric, E. F. Hutton, and Bank of Boston scandals. A June 1985 *New York Times* survey confirmed what earlier studies have shown repeatedly—the public gives business managers low marks for honesty.

Carroll goes on to write:

In this era of searching for excellence, perhaps an appropriate way to phrase the theme of my article is "Searching for the Moral Manager." Pertinent questions then became:
- Are there any?
- How many are there?
- Where are they?
- Why are they so difficult to find?

In the same issue of the publication, *Business Horizons,* published by the Indiana University Graduate School of Business, there appeared another article on corporate ethics, entitled "A CEO Looks at Ethics."

The lead sentence was, "Ethics isn't a matter of law or public relations or religion. It's a matter of trust."

This editorial went on: "The topic of ethics is an important one. It's a part of management that balances ideals against reality. During a business career, every manager can be virtually certain that he or she will have to make some rugged ethical decisions."

This editorial was written by Vernon R. Loucks, Jr., president and chief executive officer of Baxter Travenol Laboratories, Inc. Mr. Loucks summed his article up by giving four principles of ethical management. They are

1. Hire the right people.
2. Set standards more than rules.
3. Don't let yourself get isolated.
4. Let your ethical example at all times be absolutely impeccable.

He then concludes: "History shows that in the long run, the ethical course of action is the profitable course as well. This hasn't changed since 560 B.C. or so, and I don't really believe it will."

Well, we could go on and on thinking about ethics—in government, in corporations, in individuals. Ethics in organizations and government really reflect the ethics of the leaders. So there we get back to individuals.

Recent history is riddled with individuals who have shot themselves in the foot by compromising certain ethical standards. From Watergate to Irangate. From Spiro Agnew to Ivan Boesky. Jails are filled with people who valued gratification more than ethics and who ultimately paid the price. Usually it isn't a question of *knowing* what's right. Most of us know that. Rather it's a matter of *doing* what's right.

EACH OF US WILL ANSWER THIS QUESTION

There's a question that each of us will answer—either consciously or unconsciously. The question is, "What do I stand for?"

Our answers will be driven by our *values,* will reveal our *priorities,* will show our *character,* and form our *ethics.*

So, we have:

1. values,
2. priorities,
3. character, and
4. ethics.

These are all choices we make—answers to the question "What do I stand for?" The choices we make influence our success and the level of goals we reach.

SUMMING UP

Ultimately, our success and the goals we reach are determined by what we stand for—our values, priorities, character, and ethics. External circumstances don't control our lives as much as these internals.

Of course, I realize that there are many people who don't buy what I've just told you. Many would scoff at the naïveté of it. But look around you at the people who make it over the long haul. There's a consistency or integrity about the way they live their lives. To be successful, we can't long violate certain natural laws.

If you want to answer the question "What do I stand for?" you first have to distinguish between what's *temporary* and what's *permanent*. Realizing that I'm a multidimensional person helps me understand that to violate one part of my nature to satisfy another always brings problems. To violate the spiritual in order to gratify the physical sows seeds of destruction. And so it is with imbalances of any dimension.

Strong, well-established values, priorities, and ethics help us to defer gratification—to waive the temporary in favor of the permanent. This is a principle that can be applied many times in our daily lives.

One of the reasons why success is so rare is that a vast majority of people will always opt for instant gratification. But success and goal achievement demands our opting for delayed gratification in many things. That's another principle that you can apply many ways.

Enduring success has more to do with character than breaks, luck, timing, or other apparent causes of success. Enduring success comes after positive answers to these questions: "What are my values?" "What are my priorities?" "What are my ethics?"

What does all of this mean to you? How will you answer the questions I've asked in this chapter? How important do you feel they are? These questions all become part of the big question that we'll all answer, silently or loudly. And the big question is, "What do I stand for?"

11

Learning That Problems Help You Grow

People have lots of problems! You've had your share. So have I. I don't know about you, but I haven't particularly enjoyed most of mine. And yet, as I look back, I can clearly see that they were very creative experiences. I learned that I grew in proportion to the problems I met and worked through. It seems to me that our strength is consistent with the size of problems we've outmuscled.

Since I've been out of college, I've been in business for

myself. The first five years I worked for a firm, but I was on a straight commission as an outside salesman. During the twenty-eight years since then, it's been the situation that if I ate, I had to go sell something and make something happen. That's the way I like it.

But being an entrepreneur has its ups and downs. The ups have been great; some of the downs have been brutal. In my business career there have been three major defeats that gutted me so severely that it took all of the strength and resources I could possible muster just to survive them. And all three experiences, although each was separated by several years, were progressively worse.

LEARNING FROM DEFEATS

I learned a great lesson in all three of these experiences. Especially in the last one. The lesson I learned was that after each time I emerged a different person—stronger, more seasoned, viewing life from a more mature perspective and with different values.

The last of the three experiences was the roughest. It left me devastated. Our firm was marketing training courses to schools, churches, government agencies, and companies. Our problems began in the late 1970s when travel costs, hotel and food costs, and salaries skyrocketed. Suddenly, it seemed that these expenses were two or three times what they'd previously been. Our profit margins began to erode, then disappear. For a couple of years we lost more than one hundred thousand dollars each year. Sounds kind of stupid, looking back, to have allowed that to happen; but hindsight is a bit clearer than foresight. As it turned out, everything we did to correct the problem backfired and we lost money rather than making it.

Then a firm that owed us just under five hundred thousand dollars defaulted on their payments. This firm had had excellent credit for thirty years but was a victim of a sharp downturn in the automobile market. They'd overexpanded, were highly leveraged, and suddenly went broke!

We'd also expanded and spent over three hundred fifty thousand dollars producing new training programs. To finance this venture, we'd borrowed a large part of the money against the notes we held. So we woke up one day owing a bank about two hundred thousand, past due bills of about seventy-five thousand, and the IRS thirty-five thousand. And we had *no* cash!

We had to have some serious money—and have it fast. I went to work on it. First, I tried to see what we could recoup from the firm that owed us so much. They made big promises, half of which I believed, which turned out to be false expectations because they were down for the count.

Then I went back to a publishing company that had previously offered us $1 million for our firm three years previously, before we'd developed several new programs. They sensed our problems and backed off. I went to several other people who'd previously asked to invest in our firm. They picked up the same vibes and scent of trouble that the publishing company had.

In the meantime, we were getting call after call from suppliers and creditors, all, of course, wanting money. Our offices turned into a graveyard. Everybody knew we were in trouble and morale dropped through the floor.

My personal finances became critical. Fortunately, I didn't have a lot of personal debt, and more fortunately, I couldn't incur any at that time because of our company's problems. But we'd just gone through several years of having two daughters in a private college and my wife's mother in a nursing home for fifteen years. So we were really strapped.

Nothing seemed to work out. Everything I tried turned out to be a dead-end street. Weeks went by. Our problems got worse. Creditors screamed louder. Finally, we got to the point of not being able to go any further. Fear, panic, guilt, depression, and tension were a few of the emotions I felt— not to mention severe ego damage.

Then, at the last possible moment, an educational foundation showed an interest in purchasing our programs. They knew exactly the shape we were in. Their final offer was one hundred seventy-five thousand for all of our courses, records, and inventory. Seventy-five thousand in cash and a hundred thousand payable in monthly installments for three years.

We had no other choice but to sell. Over the years, we'd spent a total of well over five hundred thousand in hard dollars just in development costs, not to mention the overhead and inventory costs. It was pennies on the dollar. But we had no choice.

They came in and moved things out. Our people either quit or went with them. I was left in a big office space, with two years left on a lease, and a bunch of unused office furniture and equipment.

It took two years just to dig out. I had to begin a whole new career direction, starting from zero. Well, actually that's not correct. I did have zero dollars, but the flip side was that I owed about three hundred thousand dollars.

It was the best thing that ever happened to me! I discov-

ered strengths I never knew I had. I had to play hurt. I had
no options but to make something happen. I had the sole
responsibility of coming out; no one was around to help me.

I paid all small creditors and set up a payment schedule
with the larger ones and the IRS. It was anything but easy,
but we made progress. First the IRS was paid off, then our
creditors. I emerged a new and different person. My ego had
been beaten to a bloody pulp, and I was a lot stronger because of it. I found that I grew because of the difficulties,
whereas I probably wouldn't have if I hadn't experienced
them.

When the times were very tough, I reflected many times
on promises in the Scriptures. Such as when James wrote:
"Consider it pure joy, my brothers, whenever you face trials
of many kinds, because you know that the testing of your
faith develops perseverance. Perseverance must finish its
work so that you may be mature and complete, not lacking
anything."

Another one was in the fifth chapter of Romans: "And
we rejoice in the hope of the glory of God. Not only so, but
we also rejoice in our sufferings, because we know that suffering produces perseverance; perseverance, character; and
character, hope. And hope does not disappoint us, because
God has poured out his love into our hearts by the Holy
Spirit, whom he has given us."

Thinking about these Scriptures and knowing the pres-
ence of a Divine Power in my life gave me a feeling of
exhilaration in the midst of all of the problems and uncertainties I had.

As I said, this experience was one of the best things that
ever happened to me. I emerged a stronger person. In wrestling with and solving these big problems, I developed new

layers of mental muscle. I learned to better understand the old adage "Good judgment comes from experience, and experience comes from bad judgment."

Now, why do I share these personal struggles with you? I do so because I know that you, too, have experienced many problems or setbacks. They may not be the same as mine, but in a sense they were, in that they tested you and called for all your strength just to survive them.

I also know that many people go through life thinking that no one else has the problems that they have. I've conducted enough personal growth courses to know that most people are encouraged when they hear how others have dealt with and overcome difficulties.

Merely telling you to "hang in there" when you have tough times can be meaningless, but when I can share that advice out of my experience, rather than through mere words, the message hopefully carries more meaning.

For a moment, look back at two or three of your own challenging experiences—times when you had to muster all your strength just to cope with a problem. Didn't you become stronger as a result? Wiser? More mature? Viewed from this perspective, your problems can be very positive, creative experiences.

STRUGGLES OF FRIENDS

I'm fifty-five years old now, and as I look around at my closest friends, I see that in the last five years every one of them has experienced some of the most severe defeats of their lives.

One got into some oil deals three or four years ago, borrowing eight hundred thousand from two banks. The bank-

ers looked over the geological reports and engineering data
and enthusiastically lent him the money without any collat-
eral. It was a sure hit—everyone agreed. As it turned out, it
wasn't worth a spoon of salt water. It was a total bust, not a
nickel in return. Every dime lost.

My friend earned a good income—around a hundred
thousand a year. But figure 13 percent on eight hundred
thousand. That's right! It comes to the paltry sum of one
hundred twenty thousand a year just for interest.

He scraped everywhere he could to keep the interest payments up, until time caught up with him—as he knew it
would. Then his wife of more than thirty years got cancer
and experienced a tragic death. He felt as if someone had
taken a hunting knife and slit him open. It couldn't have
been any more devastating.

Today, he's a better person for the experiences. After losing most all of his material possessions and the love of his
life, things are looking up for him. He's remarried to a
lovely person whose spouse also had died. And while the
things he lost can never be replaced, he's finding a new life
that's exciting and fulfilling. His personal faith has changed
—it's stronger and more mature.

Another friend is an ear, nose, and throat surgeon. He
had the most successful ENT practice in this part of the
country—doing procedures that most other doctors
couldn't perform. A good money manager, he'd been wise
in the way he handled it, building up a very significant net
worth from a steady stream of income.

Then all of a sudden in the full height of his practice, he
got hit with a $2.5-million malpractice suit. He had $1 million insurance. The suit dragged on for months . . . depo-
sitions, expert medical witnesses, all kinds of legal work. It

began to really take a toll on him. In the daytime, as well as in the middle of the night, all he could think of was the possibility that a jury would rule against him and most of his net worth would be seized.

The months of worrying caused sleepless nights. For the first time in his life, he experienced depression. The emotional anguish he experienced debilitated him to the point where he could hardly function.

The thing that hurt the most was that his professional reputation was on the line. He'd dream of huge headlines in the newspaper telling the world of his lawsuit. As the trial date came nearer, his stress and trauma increased. Although it seemed like an eternity to him, the suit was finally settled before it came to trial. It was settled within what the insurance company would pay. The worst didn't happen.

My friend was left a different person than before. He was forced to sort out and analyze his own spiritual resources— to discover what was real and what had been handed to him. He has much deeper compassion for other people's problems now and has a depth that he didn't have before. His values changed. He changed. He'd tell you that he's a better person now. His problems strengthened him.

STRUGGLES CAUSE US TO REACH OUT FOR STRENGTH THAT'S GREATER THAN OUR OWN

For most of the people I know who've had struggles in their lives, the experience caused them to reach up and out for strength that's greater than their own. They've reached out for God; they've reached out for friends. Friendships and relationships are strengthened in this process. In this state, they become needed in order to make it.

I've been particularly careful to remember the people who have helped and encouraged me when I've had problems. I've especially kept my eyes open to their moments of trouble so I can pay them back. And one by one, I've seen them have problems or reversals, allowing me to be the friend to them that they've been to me. This has been extremely fulfilling.

Most of us look at our ups and downs and attempt to derive some kind of meaning or order from them. I've wondered many times why God allows seemingly bad things to happen to good people. I look at people I love and see their spouses die, have shattered dreams, experience reversals, see their children get into drugs, and other horrible problems.

I was recently sitting with a friend who'd just lost his wife. She'd had a brain tumor, had several operations, and died a slow death. They were extremely close.

As I sat in front of him, I kept thinking, "How does it feel to lose the most important thing in your life?" I was overcome with the emptiness he must have felt as well as his difficulty to see meaning in that experience. What is the meaning of suffering? Why do we have problems?

WHY DO BAD THINGS HAPPEN TO GOOD PEOPLE?

Why do bad things happen to good people? Most of us have asked this question of ourselves from time to time. I asked that of myself over and over years ago when my mother was killed in a tornado.

I got the call about five-thirty one Saturday morning. My father was in a small hospital in a town about sixty miles away. He and my mother had a travel trailer at a lake and went down there on weekends. They'd gone down this particular Friday evening, cooked some steaks out on a grill, and later went to bed.

The tornado roared through sometime after midnight, strewing people and debris for miles. At dawn the area was combed for people, and the ones still alive were taken to a small hospital. My father was able to tell the hospital attendant who he was and to call me.

I threw on some clothes and drove as quickly as I could to the hospital. Going in, I saw people and bodies lying everywhere in the small, ancient, all-but-abandoned hospital. Frantically, I asked everyone I saw about my father and mother. I finally found my father on an old operating table in this small surgical room. His right eye had been knocked out of its socket and he was severely banged up.

The doctor apologized for the lack of equipment and expertise and said because of the press of people he could only put the eye into its socket and sew it up, that it really needed a specialist, and that my father would never be able to see through it again.

I talked to my semiconscious father, who was frantically crying for my mother. No one had any idea of her whereabouts. I was allowed to examine the bodies and people awaiting treatment. She wasn't there.

It was like a battlefield. Blood everywhere. Screams. Relatives crying. Overworked nurses and doctors unable to respond to everyone's requests.

Finally, I was told to go to the funeral home, that there were some bodies there that were unidentified. I did. It was just awful. Pulling sheets off dead people's faces, not knowing what I'd find, was just about the toughest thing I'd ever done. Every part of my body throbbed. Cold sweat popped out. I was having emotional explosions inside my body that I was somehow barely able to control.

She wasn't there. Then I was allowed by the National Guard to look for her at the site of damage. It was like looking for a needle in a haystack—in all that wreckage. Nothing.

I was sent to another hospital thirty miles away. I went there. Nothing. I was going crazy. Three or four hours had gone by, which seemed like an eternity. I went back to the original hospital and funeral home. Still nothing.

In the panic of picking up all the people and bodies, none of whom had identification, they were being taken to random places. Someone suggested that I go to McLean, a small town thirty to forty miles away from the site. I did.

The funeral home in that little town had three unidentified bodies. I was allowed to look at them. And . . . there my search came to an end. I found her. It appeared that her body had been swept several hundred yards. She was mangled, mud matted in her hair. The only way I could identify her was by her wedding ring and her hairline that came down to a point on her forehead. She always called it her widow's peak.

The moment the reality that it was her hit me, I sat down and just cried like a baby. I called and made arrangements for her body to be picked up, and then went back to see about my father . . . asking myself the question "Why do bad things like this happen?"

I'm still trying to emotionally figure it out. I can only share with you what I know now—at my current stage of learning. The way I've got it figured now is that everything can be divided into what's *temporary* and what's *permanent.*

Mortal life, events, and possessions are temporary. They all pass away in time. Each of us gets old and dies. First, our hair thins, then our waistline thickens, then our faces get wrinkles, then ultimately it's us.

But the spirit that God gave us when He breathed the breath of life into us—that's permanent. That's what I believe. That's the immortality of us mortals.

I totally believe that something infinitely better awaits after this life. I fully believe that I'll take on the nature of God and enjoy the perfection that permits no illness, death, or sorrow.

I believe the promises of God along this line. I've found this thought, expressed by the Apostle Paul, helpful: "I consider that our present sufferings are not worth comparing with the glory that will be revealed in us. The creation waits in eager expectation for the sons of God to be revealed."

The beliefs that there is a Creator of this universe, and that He did create us and give us immortality, and that He designed us to pass from this life to a better one, are ones I accept. The acceptance that He offers me ultimate perfection and my own struggles help me appreciate this more, help put life's problems into a meaningful perspective for me. When push comes to shove, I've noticed that most people reach out for a higher power than themselves only when they've got problems they can't handle.

In this sense, problems help us grow. With a positive attitude, we accept them as creative growth experiences. Whether our problems are creative growth experiences or not depends on our own choices or attitudes. How we choose to view problems can strongly influence the quality of life we enjoy.

I've written down these thoughts in the hope that they will cause you to think and examine your own life. You, too, have had problems. I know you have; everyone has.

The question is, How do you react to your problems? Do they make you stronger, or do they make you weaker? Do they cause you to quit, or do they fuel you with new energy because you're determined to win over them. Do you view them as bad experiences, or do you view them as creative, growth experiences? These are important questions.

I CAN ONLY HANDLE MY PROBLEMS TODAY

The problem with problems is that we don't keep them in our todays. We drag the clutter of them with us into our tomorrows. We also reach back and pull the debris of old problems into our todays. Jesus said, "Today's problems are sufficient for today."

It's easy to be preachy about these ideas, but it's often tough to practice them. I learned a good lesson about this several years ago when conducting a goal-setting seminar in Peoria, Illinois. One of the people in attendance was a physician who was head of the hemodialysis department of St. Francis Hospital. He worked with patients who had kidney transplants and ones who were on dialysis machines.

As the three-day seminar progressed, he got excited about the possibility for his patients. After one of the sessions, he asked me, "Do you think this would be good for my patients?"

I responded, "You're the doctor, you tell me!"

He smiled and said, "Of course it would. If we could get them setting goals and getting excited about doing something before they die, rather than just waiting to die, I think it might prolong their lives."

So we set up the seminar just for his people. We had about forty to fifty, including some of their spouses. It was very difficult to conduct. Most of the people were terminal cases. They knew it; I knew it. They had no hope for a better tomorrow. Most of them had accepted death as a short-term actuality. There was a sadness about the people that I'd never experienced before.

In the seminar, they set goals. They reached the conclusion that they might not have long to live, but they could put more living into their remaining time. They released a lot of pent-up feelings in group discussions. They listened and reinforced one another. They formed support groups.

Many of the people won my heart. Once the ice was broken, they were so appreciative. I especially remember Margaret. She sat at one of the front tables. I still remember three goals she set. They were

1. to keep her kitchen clean and straight,
2. to get involved again as a Cub Scout leader, and
3. to fix herself up and maintain her physical appearance.

Not very earth-shaking goals, are they? Oh yes, they were! You see, Margaret had gone blind. She had long since been a diabetic. Her husband abandoned her when her illness progressed, leaving her with young children.

In one of the discussion sessions, I overheard her apologize to her table members for letting her attitude get bad. She explained that she'd become too self-centered and obsessed with her own problems, and how this wasn't right for her children and friends. They all rallied around her and gave her emotional support and encouragement.

What an experience! Here was a person, dying, who suddenly said, "I can be better and I can do some things to make my life more positive and enjoyable."

I wish you could have seen the transformation in her in those three days. She'd learned to use the only time frame we have to operate in—today. How many problems do we create by coughing up the problems of yesterday? And how many problems do we clutter our todays with my trying to jump ahead to our tomorrows?

MEETING AND SOLVING PROBLEMS GIVES MEANING TO LIFE

One of the paradoxes of life is that the experiences that have the power to crush us and stamp us into the ground also carry within them the potential to strengthen us and carry us to new heights of personal effectiveness.

While most of us would opt for a tensionless, blissful life, with an absence of problems, the truth is that this would be one of the worst situations that could happen to us. This is because problems and challenges call forth new levels of strength and fight that otherwise lie dormant within us.

Just as we build physical muscle by lifting weights, which challenges every bit of resistance we can muster, so do we build mental muscles by the same process . . . by being in situations that challenge every bit of our mental and spiritual capacities in order to survive them.

It is only in the process of wrestling with problems and fears that almost crush us that we put on mental muscle.

But our tendency is to avoid problems and unpleasant situations, isn't it?

In his best-selling book, *A Road Less Traveled,* M. Scott Peck writes, "This tendency to avoid problems and the emotional suffering inherent in them is the primary basis for all human mental illness." He quotes Carl Jung, who said, "Neurosis is always a substitute for legitimate suffering."

The point is well made: that our attempts to avoid suffering brings us more problems than the problems we try to dodge would have brought us. So, it's a fine line. It's neurotic to welcome and enjoy problems. It's also neurotic to avoid them. The creative way to deal with problems is to accept them head-on and courageously work them through.

It helps to look back at our lives and see how the shock, pain, and trauma of problems have helped us grow and become stronger people. In doing this, we can understand the creativity of suffering.

Suffering is creative. At least, it is when we have the appropriate attitude toward it. The appropriate attitude begins with these commitments to ourselves:

1. I'll not duck my problems, but will deal with them head-on.
2. I'll develop a living philosophy that problems help me grow.
3. I'll view suffering positively by realizing that it helps me become a better person.

Scott Peck lists the following four tools, or techniques, which, he says, help us deal with pain and suffering constructively. They are

1. delaying of gratification,
2. acceptance of responsibility,
3. dedication to truth, and
4. balancing.

A few moments or a few hours of meaningful meditation about these ideas can be a very creative experience for anyone.

SUMMING UP

Well, I've said some things in this chapter that I feel emotional about. I hope I have caused you to stop and reflect on your life experiences, and that, as you reflect, you're struck with the reality that your problems help you grow.

I hope you emotionally related to some of the stories and examples I've included, that your own emotional experiences matched some of mine. What I've written can best be learned and understood on an emotional level, not just learned intellectually.

Success is a series of ups and downs. No one has all ups. Everyone has some downs. I do. You do.

One of my mentors, W. Clement Stone, has a rather unusual response to problems. When he encounters one or when someone presents him with one, he always responds, "That's good!" He goes on to ask, "What's good about it?"

Then he begins to analyze all of the reasons why the problem is good—the positive results that might occur because the problem popped up. This is how he's learned to allow problems to help him grow.

What have you learned from your problems? How have

they helped you grow? <u>As you've fought against them, in what ways have you become stronger?</u>

<u>Problems are a fact of life.</u> You'll always have them. They can press you down or they can lift you up. It's all in how you deal with them. Remember . . . you'll grow in proportion to the size of problems you're willing to meet and work through.

12

Stretching Beyond Goal Achievement

The story is told of Alexander the Great who sat down and cried when he thought there were no more worlds to conquer. At the ripe old age of twenty-nine he achieved what no one had ever done before. And the tragedy was that, at that young age, most of his life was behind him.

You too have probably seen people reach important goals and then have nothing to live for, and either die or live an empty existence. The sad truth is that many of the goals we reach don't really satisfy us, although we think they will when we set them.

"If I can just get a better job that pays more, life's problems will all be over."

"When we get a new home with bedrooms for all of the children everything will be much better."

"If I can get a new car and trade off my old one, all my cares will be gone."

"If I can ever get out of college and get a job, I'll be happy."

"If we can only save up ten thousand dollars, we'll feel financially secure."

These and many other responses prove what most of us know anyway—that reaching material goals doesn't necessarily bring happiness and peace of mind. Then what does bring happiness?

WHAT DOES BRING HAPPINESS?

As I've observed people, it seems to me that one of our chief yearnings is to enjoy a higher state of happiness and peace of mind. Most of our material goals are really set and achieved in an attempt to push us to a greater level of contentment or enjoyment. But any serious student of human nature has observed that this doesn't work. If it did, the richest people in the world would be the happiest. They aren't. Many are miserable.

Happiness is a paradox. We find it by not seeking it. The more we seek it, the less of it we find. Our maturity confirms this mystery. Wise teachers have understood this since time began. Let's explore this paradox and see if we can develop a greater understanding of what brings us joy, contentment, and happiness . . . and what doesn't.

MUCH OF THE THRILL OF REACHING GOALS COMES IN THE STRUGGLE

As each of us gets older, this fact of life becomes more clear. The thrill of reaching goals comes more in the struggle than in the actual achievement. The moment we begin to emotionally understand this fact, a new stage of maturity begins for us.

The reason for this, I suppose, is the element of hope. Dreaming, planning, fantasizing about reaching goals is, in some ways, better than reaching them. Hope has magic that reality doesn't. Hope is associated with things good. It isn't encumbered with bad.

But as we think about hope, we can see a couple of problems. First, some people get their kicks out of setting and planning goals, so they see no need to struggle and do what it takes to reach them. On the other hand, there are still others who don't enjoy the journey of reaching their goals. They live anxiously in their tomorrows, not allowing their todays to be exciting, adventurous, and fulfilling.

Mature people commit themselves to goals *and* enjoy the process of reaching them. They feel responsibility, while at the same time enjoying the rewards of their efforts.

Maybe you don't need advice along this line, but I do. One of my weaknesses is that I get so uptight and determined to get something done that often I don't enjoy the trip. When I was in college, I couldn't wait to get out, get married, and get a job. Then I couldn't wait to get my own business . . . and so on. I have to work on this constantly.

WE DON'T TAKE TIME TO ENJOY GOALS WE REACH

This is an observation I've made about people.

I read a story a few years ago about the legendary Vince Lombardi. His wife told how one year, when the Green Bay Packers had won the Super Bowl and all of the players and coaches were celebrating the victory with trips, parties, and accolades, Lombardi got up early the next morning, went to his office, and began looking at game films. He was preparing for the next year. He couldn't allow himself to stop and enjoy the moment—not even for one day.

On the other hand, I know people who reach goals and then enjoy them so much that they never get around to setting any more. So their lives are behind them.

I once had a friend whose glory days were when he was a high school athlete. As a football star in his hometown, he got tremendous recognition from everyone there. On Saturday mornings, after games on Friday evenings, he'd walk down the main street and all of the merchants would flock around him, praising him and telling him how great he was. He enjoyed this immensely, as most people would.

The problem was that he peaked out at that young age. Never again did he set and achieve goals that excited him. He spent his life looking back, and feeling guilty doing so. His life was always behind him. Most of his living had already been done.

Do you take time to enjoy the goals you reach? Do you take time to enjoy the thrill of victory? Do you allow yourself the time and emotions to savor your achievements? It's creative to do so, even though that can be carried to an extreme.

But still there's something more important than reaching tangible goals.

STRETCHING BEYOND GOAL ACHIEVEMENT

Several years ago I had a conference with a man whom I'd never met before. I was to do a training session for his company and we met at the Admirals Club in the American Airlines terminal at Dallas–Fort Worth airport.

As we discussed the seminar, I explained that one subject we covered was developing support systems. He showed some interest in this subject and asked me several questions about what we did. I explained that I defined the concept of support systems as developing relationships with a few people for the purpose of helping one another reach goals.

I went on to explain that a support system is a relationship that anyone can structure, and that it should be characterized by total openness and total trust. I told them that in this mutually supportive relationship a synergistic force was formed that was greater than the sum of the individuals' abilities. I explained that in this relationship, where the whole is greater than the sum of the parts, each person benefits by gaining greater strength and creative abilities.

He had several questions that I responded to. He asked me if I had such an association with others, and I said yes and told him about them. I could see he had some deep, perplexing thoughts within him.

In a moment, he blurted out, "It would be impossible for me to do anything like that!" I asked why.

"Because I don't know anyone who'd have anything in common with me . . . I'm worth fifty million dollars!"

I looked at him for a moment and finally thought of

something to say. "Is money all that you want to have in common with people?"

He thought for a few seconds and gushed out something that must have been very difficult for him to admit. He said, "Frankly, I don't have a friend in the world—no one who'd be close enough to do what you're describing." He paused again and then added, "There're probably only two people in the whole world that really love me—my two young children. My wife doesn't; my older children don't!"

He seemed resigned to this state. But then, a few seconds after he opened up and said what he had said, he closed up like a steel trap and kept me well at arm's length. I suspect he regretted his sudden burst of openness.

What a tragedy, I told myself. I felt like telling him that there's a simple solution to his problem. Give his $50 million to charities, keeping only enough to take his family on a long vacation where he did nothing but patch up their relationships.

The man had obviously achieved some high financial goals but found that they left him with a void. He had no idea what real happiness and self-fulfillment were all about. He was in a trap that would release him only if his priorities and values changed. I suspected they never would. Many others have the same problem.

HAPPINESS IS A SERENDIPITY

Over twenty years ago, J. Wallace Hamilton wrote a great little book entitled *Serendipity.* He used this exciting word to make several points about life and living. He described serendipity as an unexpected outcome that happens quite by accident when we're in pursuit of something else.

He began by telling how many modern-day inventions are the result of discoveries made while attempting to discover something totally different. His major point was that we all find happiness quite by accident—by a process of indirection. The paradox, he pointed out, is that if we set a goal to be happy, contented, or fulfilled, and seek it directly, we'll not find it. It's only when we strike out on a selfless mission that we discover genuine happiness. He drove home the point that the things we do to achieve happiness usually backfire on us and keep us from enjoying the very thing we seek.

The happiest people I know are people who are very busy using their talents, doing what they enjoy doing, contributing to the happiness of others. The most unhappy people I know are the ones who are pushing, shoving, clawing, and grabbing everything they can for themselves.

Again, the paradox of happiness, contentment, or self-fulfillment is that we don't get it by directly going after it. It's a process of indirection—a serendipity. This doesn't mean that happiness comes as an accident. It doesn't. It has definite causes.

What are the causes of happiness? It seems to me as I've observed people—happy ones and unhappy ones—that these are some of the key ingredients of happiness:

1. accepting ourselves as we are and accepting others as they are,
2. accepting God's acceptance of us, and
3. allowing others to accept us as we are.

One of my objectives is to challenge you to set goals in these dimensions. These can be self-actualizing goals, ones that take you to new heights of self-fulfillment. These are not goals for things but ones that get you outside yourself.

ACCEPTING OURSELVES AS WE ARE
AND ACCEPTING OTHERS AS THEY ARE

One of our great thinkers of modern years is Carl Rogers. In reading his writings several years ago, I read something that struck me like lightning. He wrote, "When I accept myself as I am, I change. When I accept others as they are, they change!"

I adopted that as a whole training philosophy. And I discovered that it works. I've trained more than sixteen thousand instructors to conduct my sales and personal development courses for several hundred thousand people, and some of the main guidelines we ask them to follow are these: Completely, totally accept every person enrolled in the course—regardless of how they act or respond, and look for strengths and assets in each individual—give positive reinforcement as often as possible.

We've found that these actions work miracles in people. It helps them accept themselves so that their hidden abilities can surface. This paradox—that we change when we accept ourselves, and we change others by accepting them—is quite the opposite of human nature. Sometimes I'm mature enough to do it; other times I'm not. I often forget to do it, although I've seen it work many times.

Early in my training career I remember Dr. Maxwell Maltz telling a story to me. A teacher at a special education school for children had applied the principles of his book *Psycho-Cybernetics* to her curriculum.

One youngster about ten years old was so socially withdrawn that he wouldn't talk to anyone other than his immediate family. He was enrolled in this school, although he wouldn't talk to the teacher or the other kids. The boy wouldn't participate, or play with the other kids. He showed absolutely no ability to communicate.

The teacher understood that it was the boy's inner self-image that had to change before his outer behavior could change. She had no idea what had happened in his past to cause his present condition to exist. And she didn't care. She was looking to the future.

So she totally accepted him. However he wanted to act, as long as it wasn't destructive, was acceptable. She never missed a chance to reinforce him. Any effort he made was quickly reinforced by her. She communicated her positive expectations to him as often as she could.

At first, nothing happened. He didn't respond. Then, after a while, she began to notice very slight responses that indicated that she might possibly be getting through to him. All this time he never said a word. Days went by. Weeks went by.

One day while all the other kids were outside playing she went back into the classroom to check on him. He was alone. She watched him from a position where he couldn't see her. When other kids were around, he never moved or showed any interest in them or their work. As she watched him now, he was busy inspecting the work the kids had hung on the bulletin boards.

The teacher watched him for a few minutes and then walked into the classroom. When she did, she startled him, and instinctively he blurted out, almost screaming, "Where are those damn kids?"

She was stunned. He talked! She grabbed him and hugged

him and told him how proud of him she was. Before long he began talking and playing with the other kids.

Do you think that teacher experienced a full jolt of joy and happiness? Of course! Did it make her any extra money? Probably not! Was she a pretty mature, self-actualized person? It certainly sounds like she was! Do you see a clue for happy living in this story?

A SPIRITUAL EXPERIENCE?

I've observed that when I accept other people as they are, what happens inside me is closely akin to a spiritual experience. I've also noticed it in others. In training courses when I first model total acceptance and class members begin to accept others as they are, they enjoy somewhat of a spiritual experience, too. I wish I understood this dynamic more.

Several years ago, every day for six months, I read the book of I John in the bible. I was particularly struck with passages like: "God is love. Whoever lives in love lives in God, and God in him."

What is this dynamic called love, I asked myself over and over. It sounded so simple . . . it sounded so complex! Again, we deal in paradoxes, seeming contradictions.

One great paradox is the spiritual change, the transformation that occurs when we accept ourselves as we are. Most of us don't, you know. Instead we have guilt, anxiety, remorse, feelings of inferiority, and other self-defeating attitudes.

Here's where religions often fail us. Often they impose rules and regulations that always make us feel weak and ineffective. Often they bind us and put emotional strangleholds on us. They can reinforce our guilt, causing our self-images to be ones of inadequacy.

Now, before you take issue with me, let me explain what I mean when I say "religion." I simply refer to any system of rules and regulations that make our own actions, and our own goodness, the sole determinant of our value.

The only solution comes when we understand God's true nature—that of love and total acceptance. Because of my acceptance of God's promises, I can have confidence in His looking past my blemishes and totally accepting me. As I emotionally internalize this belief, I change. I change because I now see me as adequate.

This act of faith regenerates me and I become a different person. I can feel accepted by a perfect being. I can be accepted as perfect even though I'm imperfect. All this can happen when God's spirit dwells in me. (I'll write more of this later in this chapter.)

Again, one of our greatest needs is the need for acceptance. We need acceptance from people. We need acceptance from a higher power. When this need is filled we live happier lives. When it isn't, our lives can be empty. It's in this dynamic of acceptance that we change and grow.

ACCEPTANCE CHANGES PEOPLE

I've seen what appeared to be mean, hostile people change when I gave them prolonged doses of acceptance and positive reinforcement. I also felt something inside myself change when I did.

I'll never forget a course I began many years ago. In the first session, I asked each person to tell the others why they enrolled in the course and what they wanted to gain from it.

About halfway through it a man, whose first name was George, gruffly gave me this response. With arms tightly folded, he said, "I don't want to gain anything from this course . . . I don't even want to be in it! And I wouldn't be if I wasn't told that I *had* to come!"

As he spewed out these words, he looked right at me, defying me to cross him. Immediately, all heads snapped around to me to see how I was going to handle that.

I leaned forward, looked George squarely in his right eyeball, smiled as broadly as I could, and said, "George, thank you for what you've just said. For being honest with me." I paused a moment to allow that to sink in. Then I continued, "George, this is a course where you can be totally honest . . . and be totally accepted." Again I paused. He looked totally confused. I went on, "So, would you do me a favor?"

He responded skeptically, "What is it?"

"Would you continue to be honest with us? Would you continue to say exactly what you feel? Would you do that?"

He skeptically eyed me for a moment and then said, "Yeah, yeah, I'll do it!" Saying this, he gave his head a quick nod up and down.

And guess what? He began to change at that exact moment. And in the nine weeks of the course, he changed dramatically. The real, beautiful person that had been bottled up within that gruff exterior came out, and he experienced a level of happiness that he hadn't had in many years. And I enjoyed it, too.

In another class I conducted, a young man was enrolled who showed as much hostility as I'd ever seen before. The first two or three sessions he wore a huge fur-lined Eskimo parka to class . . . and kept it on throughout the two-hour sessions. Not only that—but he wore fur-lined leather mit-

tens that were as big as boxing gloves. He would sit in the
front row and pull the hood of the parka up over his head.
Man, it was weird!

Obviously, he was trying to get me to slap him on his
wrist and scold him like a little child. His antics broke up
the class the first couple of sessions. When it came his time
to make his weekly presentation, he'd stand at the front of
the room all hunkered down in the jacket, peer out at everyone through the opening in the hood, make smart-aleck re-
marks, and then sit down.

I'd then walk to the front of the class with the purpose of
making a positive, reinforcing remark to him. Man, did that
test my creativity!

The score the first three weeks was 3 to 0. He was holding
a commanding lead in the win column. I kept acting as if
nothing was the least bit irregular. Each week I accepted
him however he wanted to act and tried to point out a
strength I noticed in him.

About the fifth week he came to class . . . and guess
what? He didn't have the Eskimo coat on or the mittens. It
came time for him to stand and make a talk to the class, and
I knew something was about to happen.

He stood at the front with a serious look on his face. He
tried to speak . . . and nothing came out. He couldn't say
a word. I watched him like a hawk and instinctively knew
that his emotions were about to blow. After a few seconds,
when no words came out of his mouth, he ran down the
center aisle and out of the classroom in total embarrassment.

As he ran by me, I could see heavy trauma exploding
inside him. I quickly turned and whispered to a class mem-

ber, "Go find him, stay with him until he calms down, and bring him back." I went ahead conducting the class.

In about fifteen minutes, they both came back into the room, the young man looking as if he'd been run over by a steamroller. Embarrassed, he didn't even look at me. I'm sure it took all the strength he had to come back and stay.

I didn't make a big deal of his experience, just patted him on his back and in a quiet voice told him to sit down. I then went on conducting the class as if nothing had happened. Then, in about six to eight minutes, I looked directly at him and in a soft, yet definite voice, said his name and then said, "Please come back up and finish your presentation."

He did. And the story he finally told was a classic. After he got going, he told of being born to parents who were up in years. As I recall, he said his father was in his sixties.

He told about his childhood. He told how his father never did anything with him: never played with him, never took him camping or fishing or to ball games. He painfully told how he grew up hating his father for what he'd deprived him of. As he told this story, his emotions just drained out of him. The years of bitterness, hatred, and fear came spewing out of him like air being released from a giant balloon.

He told that his plans had been to leave home when he was eighteen. And he did. In the middle of his talk, he began to bog down again. I knew that something pretty heavy was about to come out. I could just sense that he hadn't told everything that he needed to tell.

Slowly, painfully, he told us that a few weeks earlier he had received a call from a nurse at a hospital, who said his father was there, dying. She said that his father had asked them to find him and get him to come see him before he died.

In his early twenties, when he told the story, he said that he'd never gone back to see his father since he left home a few years earlier. He told of the resentment that had built up.

The young man told about going to the hospital. Filled with conflicting emotions of fear, resentment, dread, anxiety, he went into the room where his father lay. He painfully went to the bedside, took his father's hand, and stood there trying to get up the courage to tell him that he loved him and didn't really hate him, but his words wouldn't come out. His father died before the young man could speak.

He left that scene so devastated by guilt and remorse that he hated the world. He hated himself; he hated everyone else. I later found that there was reason to suspect that he had physically abused his wife.

But in that session that day I saw a human being go through a total transformation—right before my eyes. It was cataclysmic, with all of the force of emotion of a volcano erupting, following by an incredible peace and calm.

As he finished, I went to the front, hugged him, and let him know that his behavior was totally appropriate, that he was completely accepted by me and the class members. And we had a prayer for him.

I saw him a few years later. He had become a minister. He looked great. He looked happy, and his wife looked particularly happy. I found out that he was well adjusted and doing a good job for the church he was serving.

In the training courses I've personally conducted, as well as the ones that several thousand of our instructors have conducted, I've seen the same thing happen to many, many people. Their lives changed when they felt totally accepted.

THE PARADOX OF PERSONAL GROWTH

The paradox is that as these changes happened to our students, our instructors enjoyed the serendipity. Their lives also changed in the process. While going into the training courses with no agenda to make ourselves look good but totally focusing on the students, our lives have been supercharged with greater enthusiasm and vitality.

After observing these changes for twenty-five years now, I don't know any way to describe the dynamic other than the fact that it's a spiritual change in people; not religious but spiritual. Something happens in their inner beings.

ACCEPTING GOD'S ACCEPTANCE OF US

As I understand the purpose of Christianity more, it seems to me that the essence is to provide a direct way for us to enjoy total acceptance of the Creator. This view, as opposed to the view that God is a vengeful power that sits somewhere above us handing out punishment when we're bad (which we always are), frees us and makes us feel alive and valuable.

But what a tough task to emotionally understand how a perfect being could accept an imperfect one! It's in the sticky thornbed of the human condition that Christianity offers the most. It simply says that the man Jesus Christ came to the world two thousand years ago to show humankind what God is like. He performed miracles and left tangible evidence that he was who he said he was.

His message was simple, "Believe that I'm who I say I am and put your future on this belief, and you'll be given the

Spirit of God to dwell in you—and you'll inherit something
I call Eternal Life!"

In this act of faith we do change. As we understand it
more and accept it more, we'll change more.

The problem, again, is to emotionally understand how a
perfect being can accept me when I don't even accept me.
And I know me. How could someone like me be accepted
when I willfully do crummy things—*knowing* I'm doing
crummy things? And if I do forgive myself, I can't enjoy the
guilt that reinforces my low self-esteem? And on . . . and
on.

If you're waiting for answers to all these questions, I'm
afraid you'll be disappointed. I'd love to straighten all this
out for you, but I'm still trying to sort it out myself.

I have observed that we can best understand and internalize God's acceptance of us by accepting others, also by for-
giving others. These actions aren't just nice little rules of
conduct to win friends and influence people. They emotionally teach us the nature of God. And let me emphasize that
this isn't just an intellectual experience, but rather an emotional one. To understand the power and cleansing of forgiveness, we have to experience it emotionally. It's not
something we know or learn it's something we do and experience.

The times I have—face to face—told someone that they
have offended me but that I forgive them and totally accept
them, have been great growth experiences. But the times
someone has told me that they forgive me have been much
greater growth experiences.

In the emotional experience of accepting others we can
better understand God's acceptance of us. We change; others change. As I've attempted to understand what and why

and how these changes take place in people, I can only conclude that we are spiritual beings and that certain activities affect spiritual changes in us. Again, paradoxes. Serendipities.

ALLOWING OTHERS TO ACCEPT US AS WE ARE

This may be the toughest of all! Why? Because when we don't accept ourselves as we are and don't feel accepted by a Higher Power, it's difficult to allow others to accept us. Many people even unconsciously engineer rejection from others because of their own low self-esteem.

Think about it for a moment. Most antisocial behavior—such as defensiveness, aggression, bad temper, and a host of other offenses—is the manifestation of this inability (or unwillingness) to allow others to accept us as we are.

We wear masks, we play roles, we put on façades. And as I said, carried to an extreme, we even engineer rejection at times . . . all because we're afraid to reveal who we are and allow others to accept us. But think of the people you like to be around, and you'll discover people who are usually open, honest, and who assume your acceptance. They allow you to accept them.

I learned a great lesson about this around twenty years ago from a person who became a very good friend. Syd Wyatt was a minister who should have been a tennis pro. One of the most open, honest people I've ever met, he was good medicine for a person like me who'd grown up to be pretty closed. The first time we met I could tell he really liked me. The reason I knew was that he told me he did, like a big puppy dog.

He was very spontaneous about everything. He'd come by my office, stick his feet on my desk, and visit. We'd play handball at the YMCA. He was a maniac. He hated to lose and would do anything to win—including screaming to mess up my shots, blocking me, lying about calls, kneeing and elbowing me, hitting me in the back with a shot to keep me loose and ruin my concentration.

The man was a maniac! Through all the play, he badgered, cajoled, and chortled—thoroughly enjoying himself. Then after we finished playing, he'd shower, halfway dry off, and lie down on the dressing room floor—spread-eagled in his birthday suit in front of a fan. There he'd replay, regale, and chirp about the number he'd done on me. Then he'd put his socks and shoes on and chug-a-lug a couple bottles of Big Red soda pop. He always lost his car keys, so I'd have to take him home to get a spare set—which his wife always kept on hand.

What a character. From him I learned lying, cheating, physical abuse, and dirty playing—all virtues, of course, that a minister is supposed to teach his flock! There was never any doubt that he loved me like a brother. His friendship was a special thing. He loved people and instinctively allowed people to accept him as he was.

THE STRUGGLE FOR SELF-ACCEPTANCE

As a student of human nature, as well as a struggler, it's my opinion that one of our core problems is simply lack of self-acceptance. It's a common, natural problem. It's also a spiritual problem. We get it from the struggles of life. Most people suffer from it to various degrees. I do. You do. We do because for some reason we tend to focus on our weaknesses more than we do on our strengths.

I've never shaken off all the deep insecurities that were permanently creased in me during my childhood and teenage years by a father who was harsh and critical. In the forty-five years of my life while he lived, I never once remember him praising me or complementing me or approving of me.

In my growing-up years, I deeply resented him. In my young adult years, I distanced myself from him and was determined to be successful, where he wasn't. In my midadult years, I came to understand it all and forgave him. But even with understanding and knowing "why," some of the effects still remain.

Do you relate to this? Most of us do because we've all experienced similar things. No, maybe not with a parent, but with some other person or circumstance that bang us around and causes us to view ourselves as inadequate. It takes a lot of maturity to accept ourselves as we are. It does because there's so much evidence that we're not as good as we "should" be.

Today, I see a lot of people attempt to gain self-acceptance by focusing on themselves—making self-acceptance their aim. But, in doing this, they jam up their mechanism and compound their problem of nonacceptance. Self-acceptance isn't gained by directly seeking it. Again, that's a paradox of life: a serendipity. It comes as we focus on something or someone else. It comes in the pursuit of helping others, serving God, getting involved in something *outside* ourselves. It's that simple. It's that difficult.

So, to recap—self-acceptance comes after these indirect actions:

1. by accepting ourselves as we are and others as they are,
2. by accepting God's acceptance of us, and
3. by allowing others to accept us as we are.

SETTING GOALS TO GET OUTSIDE YOURSELF

What goals can you set that will get you outside yourself? What can you do to contribute to the well-being of others? What can you do to create value for others? What can you do to help other people see themselves as better people? These are extremely important questions to answer . . . and not to just answer but to set productive goals for their attainment.

Some of the happiest moments of my life have been times when I was able to help someone without any thought of reward or appreciation. To help someone who couldn't give me anything in return or who wouldn't even know who gave it to them.

One of the great books that I read, which strongly influenced me, was one written by David Dunn many years ago. It's called *Try Giving Yourself Away* (published by Prentice-Hall). In it, Dunn convincingly writes about reaching the elusive goal of happiness. His whole message is that happiness, joy, and contentment come by giving ourselves away rather than accumulating.

The book is so fresh, so timely, so true that reading it brings a feeling of freshness and wellness. Then when some of his suggestions are practiced, these positive emotions are intensified. Go to the trouble of ordering the book. You'll love it.

What goals can you set that will get you outside yourself?

Are you willing to take the time and the risk to do it? All
that's at stake is your future happiness!

SUMMING UP

Let me summarize this chapter with these thoughts:

1. There's much more to life than just reaching material
   goals—they don't bring real happiness anyway.
2. Often the struggles to reach goals produce more happiness and vitality than reaching them—we should also
   take time to enjoy the journey of reaching the goals.
3. Happiness is a serendipity—it comes not by directly
   seeking it but in a process of getting outside ourselves.
4. Maturity comes when we're able to accept others as
   they are and accept ourselves as we are—in this process we touch spiritual dimensions.
5. Self-acceptance and acceptance of God's acceptance
   help us allow others to accept us.
6. Real happiness comes as a result of setting goals to get
   outside ourselves.

Goals! What an interesting subject! I hope I have helped
you to understand them more. To understand exactly what
they are, how to reach them, and how to reach higher, self-
actualized goals.

AFTERWORD

The Goal Achievement System I've presented in this book can work for any kind of goals you want to set—material ones as well as higher, spiritual ones. I'm incredibly thrilled about sharing these ideas with you, thrilled about what can happen in your life. It delights me to think about the goals and new levels of living that you might enjoy when you follow the guidelines I've given you.

My address is in this book. I'd love to hear from you about the results you experience when you apply these ideas. So . . . thank you for reading this book and for *assimilating* and *applying* the principles in it. The possibility of our working together to help you get more living out of life is a exhilarating one. I'm indeed thankful to the Creator for the gift of life and for the opportunity to share these observations with you.

May you reach many worthwhile goals!

Bibliography

Dunn, David. *Try Giving Yourself Away.* Englewood Cliffs, N.J.:
    Prentice-Hall, 1947.
Hamilton, J. Wallace. *Serendipity.* Westwood, N.J.: Fleming H.
    Revell, 1965.
Hill, Napoleon. *The Law of Success.* Chicago, Ill.: Combined Reg-
    istry, 1937.
Hill, Napoleon. *Think and Grow Rich.* New York: Fawcett Crest,
    1960.

Maltz, Maxwell. *Psycho-Cybernetics.* Englewood Cliffs, N.J.: Prentice-Hall, 1960.

Peck, M. Scott. *A Road Less Traveled.* New York: Simon & Schuster, 1978.

Peters, Tom, and Nancy Austin. *A Passion for Excellence.* New York: Random House, 1985.

Pickens, T. Boone. *Boone.* Boston: Houghton Mifflin, 1987.

Stone, W. Clement, and Napoleon Hill. *Success Through a Positive Mental Attitude.* Englewood Cliffs, N.J.: Prentice-Hall, 1960.

WANT TO USE THIS BOOK WITH STUDY GROUPS?

A special leader's guide for effective study groups is available. This guide structures thirteen weekly meetings. The format is for one-hour discussion groups and helps each participant to assimilate and apply the concepts in each chapter.

This special ring binder makes the role of discussion leader an easy, productive one.

The price of the study guide is twenty-five dollars, plus two fifty for postage and handling. To order, send check to:

> Ron Willingham
> P. O. Box 8190
> Amarillo, TX 79114

When you order this study guide, you will also receive, *free of charge,* a personally autographed copy of this book.

ABOUT THE AUTHOR

Ron Willingham is chairman of SalesTraining, Inc., a firm specializing in sales and customer service training. Well over five hundred thousand people have graduated from his courses, in such companies as Chevrolet, Metropolitan Life Insurance Company, Avis Car Rental, and many more. More than sixteen thousand instructors have been certified to conduct his courses in banks, chambers of commerce, colleges, and companies.

He wrote the *first* personal development program ever produced on audiocassettes, has written five books and over twenty training courses conducted in all fifty states and several foreign countries.

He is the author of *Integrity Selling: How to Succeed in Selling in the Competitve Years Ahead.*